ISSUES IN POLITICAL THEORY

Political Theory has undergone a remarkable development in recent years. From a state in which it was once declared dead, it has come to occupy a central place in the study of Politics. Both political ideas, and the wide-ranging arguments to which they give rise, are now treated in a rigorous, analytical fashion, and political theorists have contributed to disciplines as diverse as economics, sociology and law. These developments have made the subject more challenging and exciting, but they have also added to the difficulties of students and others coming to the subject for the first time. Much of the burgeoning literature in specialist books and journals is readily intelligible only to those who are already well-versed in the subject.

Issues in Political Theory is a series conceived in response to this situation. It consists of a number of detailed and comprehensive studies of issues central to Political Theory which take account of the latest developments in scholarly debate. While making original contributions to the subject, books in the series are written especially for those who are new to Political Theory. Each volume aims to introduce its readers to the intricacies of a fundamental political issue and to help them find their way through the detailed, and often complicated, argument that this issue has attracted.

PETER JONES
ALBERT WEALE

ISSUES IN POLITICAL THEORY

Series editors: PETER JONES and ALBERT WEALE

Published

Christopher J. Berry: **Human Nature**
Michael Lessnoff: **Social Contract**
Richard Lindley: **Autonomy**
Andrew Reeve: **Property**

Forthcoming

David Beetham: **Legitimacy**
Tom Campbell: **Justice**
Tim Gray: **Freedom**
John Horton: **Political Obligation**
Peter Jones: **Rights**
Susan Mendus: **Toleration and the Limits of Liberty**
Raymond Plant: **Equality**
Hillel Steiner: **Utilitarianism**

Property

Andrew Reeve

HUMANITIES PRESS INTERNATIONAL, INC.
ATLANTIC HIGHLANDS, NJ

First published in 1986 in the United States of America by
HUMANITIES PRESS INTERNATIONAL, INC., Atlantic Highlands, NJ 07716

LIBRARY OF CONGRESS CATALOGING IN PUBLICATION DATA

Reeve, Andrew.
   Property.
   (Issues in political theory)
   Bibliography: p.
   Includes index.
   1. Right of property. I. Title. II. Series.
JC505.R44   1986   323.4'6   86-7187
ISBN 0-391-03438-3
ISBN 0-391-03437-5 (pbk.)

PRINTED IN HONG KONG

For my mother

Contents

Acknowledgements

My interest in the political theory of property began with a postgraduate project concerned with the seventeenth century. I remain indebted to a number of individuals and institutions who helped me to pursue it – especially Mr Keith Thomas, the Fellows of Nuffield College and the Social Science Research Council. My colleagues at Warwick have sharpened my appreciation of the complexities of the subject by their candid criticism and by their ability to draw on an extensive – and sometimes esoteric – range of material. I am also grateful to friends in Edinburgh, whose hospitality I enjoyed while planning this book. Participants in seminars at Edinburgh, Manchester, Lancaster and Birmingham helped me with their comments. John Cunliffe and Timothy Kenyon subjected earlier versions to careful and incisive criticism. I am also grateful to the editors for their help and encouragement. While these friends have increased the pleasures of exploring an issue in political theory, I would not wish to implicate them in responsibility for what follows.

ANDREW REEVE

1   Introduction

In the middle of the nineteenth century, the political economist J. R. McCulloch wrote a book about the law of inheritance and succession. He was interested in the various ways in which property might be passed from one generation to the next, and in identifying the changes which had occurred in such practices historically. He drew his examples from Greek, Roman and European legal systems, aiming to identify the impact of these different ways of regulating inheritance on (what he called) 'the public interests'. By that phrase, he seems to have understood 'economic performance', using that to determine the 'best' way to regulate inheritance. It might be thought, then, that McCulloch would have to face the prior question of whether the system of private property which allowed for inheritance was itself desirable. But he raised the question only to move on impatiently:

> 'It is not necessary in prosecuting an enquiry of this sort to take up the reader's time by entering into any statements explanatory of the advantages resulting from the establishment of a right of private property. These are obvious, and have been universally admitted. Till such right has been established there can be neither industry nor civilisation . . . The utility, or rather necessity, of securing to every individual the peaceable enjoyment of the produce he has raised, and of the ground he has cultivated and improved, is so very evident that it must have been perceived at the first institution of society.' (1848, pp.2–3)

In the very same year in which McCulloch published his essay, one political group was making it very clear that the advantages of a right of private property were by no means 'universally admitted'. The Communist Party aimed at the abolition of bourgeois private property, which was taken to be the 'final and most complete expression' of a class system of production and exploitation:

> 'In this sense, the theory of the Communists may be summed up in one sentence: Abolition of private property.
>
> We Communists have been reproached with the desire of abolishing the right of personally acquiring property as the fruit of a man's own labour, which property is alleged to be the groundwork of all personal freedom, activity, and independence.'

But, the *Manifesto* maintains,

> 'Communism deprives no man of the power to appropriate the products of society; all that it does is to deprive him of the power to subjugate the labour of others by means of such appropriation.' (McLellan, 1977, pp.232–3)

McCulloch saw self-evident and universally admitted advantages in private property, but the Communists saw only benefits for the bourgeoisie at the expense of the proletariat. Where McCulloch praised private property rights for securing to an individual the fruits of his labour, the Communists denied that the fruits of all labour were thereby secured – and identified private property with the circumstances of exploitation.

The contrast between these two positions, one of which regards private property as an undeniable advantage, the other of which claims that property is an enemy of social harmony, is not, of course, original to the nineteenth century. Plato had argued for common property when he specified the arrangements to be made for the Guardians of his ideal republic, and Aristotle had argued against Plato's conception of the place of property in social relations. Obviously, between Plato's time, and McCulloch's, one can find many advocates of arguments for and against private property. Although it is no doubt true that one major issue in political theory has been the rival merits of private property and common (or public or state) property, to merely list the arguments put on both sides would not carry us very far, for three reasons.

First, we need an understanding of the concepts of property which are employed when the merits of different property systems are under discussion. We must explore what is meant by 'private property', 'common property', 'public ownership' and so on. If we feel inclined to complain of the breeziness with which McCulloch assumes the self-evidence of the desirability of private property, we might equally complain that he assumes an understanding of what 'private property' means. But we shall find that 'property' is not an easy concept to elucidate, as Renée Hirschon discovered in an anthropological study:

> 'Inevitably for us as westerners [our notions of property] are rooted in our own particular historical experience. Broadly speaking, our attitudes to property are associated with the development of capitalism and with the notion of the commodity. Property for us is based on the idea of "private ownership" which confers on the individual the right to use and disposal . . . But what we take for granted – the idea of an individual actor having defined rights *vis-à-vis* others, and the notion of property as consisting in objects or things – is far from being universal. On the contrary these concepts are historically and culturally situated in the western tradition. This very familiarity may blind us to fundamental differences in concepts of "property" and "persons" in other social groups.' (Hirschon, 1984, p.2)

This conceptual problem, concerned with the meaning or meanings of 'property', will be explored in Chapter 2.

Hirschon's remarks also suggest the second reason for the inadequacy of listing arguments for and against private property; she draws attention to the historical dimension of our present notions. The view that our ideas of property and ownership are connected with the historical experience of capitalism has been developed within political theory, and is used by one writer as an argument for the inadequacy of liberal political thought which is alleged to rely upon a flawed notion of property. This thesis is addressed in Chapter 3, which deals with debate about the 'history' of property. The historical context in which ideas about property were put forward constitutes our second reason for supposing that a simple listing of arguments for and against private property would be unhelpful. The economic and political framework in which ideas are placed is an important consideration when we come to assess their merit, and the nature of the economies a particular theorist was in a position to know about is crucial both to the coherence of his ideas and to their relevance for us. Although Plato, Winstanley and Marx all favoured common property, the institutional frameworks within which they proposed to realise their recommendations were quite different, not least because only Marx had the historical experience of developed capitalism before him.

The third reason for dissatisfaction with a list of arguments for and against private property is that there is no reason to commit ourselves exclusively to 'private' or 'common' property. We might decide that the most desirable arrangement requires common property in some 'things' or resources, and private property in others. The institution of property is not only historically varied, it is also extremely flexible. For example, we might accept that private property should be recognised, yet reject the idea that property may be transmitted to the next generation by the will of its present owner. The flexibility of property as an institution is explored in the next two chapters.

Hirschon is undoubtedly right to suggest that we are inclined to take ideas about property for granted. Most citizens of modern Western states do not give much attention to their attitudes to the foundations of property. Their political outlook may suggest reasons why they favour a particular mix of private and public ownership, for wishing to extend or diminish the scope of markets, or for aiming at a particular distribution of income or wealth. But, in this ordinary way, few will pause to ask why anyone should be thought to own anything at all, why property of any kind is desirable, or on what grounds they would assert their entitlement to what they call 'their own'.

This unreflecting attitude may, however, sometimes be challenged. People are often surprised when their expectations about their property turn out to be unfulfilled. Someone whose goods have been stolen may be amazed to discover that the police will not necessarily return his property, even when they have discovered its whereabouts, advising him instead to take private legal action to repossess it. Again, a landowner upon whom a compulsory purchase order is served may be dismayed not only because he has no wish to sell his land, but also because the valuation offered disappoints him. Finally, two people who have lived together, or at least one of them, may blanch at the law's decision about the disposition of the goods they have acquired, when their relationship breaks up acrimoniously.

Of course, this suggests merely that the details of the legal regulation of property may be unknown to many of the persons who are governed by it. But the point goes a little deeper. In circumstances like these, the disaffected property owner is likely to give reasons for his disappointment; 'I would never have allowed Joe to move in if I thought he'd end up with half the house'; 'I used to think this was my land, but the local authority can insist I sell it to them'. This soon leads to reasoning about the rights over things which people *should* enjoy, and this is reasoning about how the law *should* operate, providing the considerations which make a particular structure of property rights desirable.

A second challenge to an unreflecting attitude comes to the fore with the experience of suffering theft or robbery. People who have returned home to discover that they have been robbed report a particular psychological reaction to the experience, quite distinct from the material loss and the emotional unpleasantness of finding their property in disarray. Rather, two other aspects of the experience are of interest here. There is first the notion that some objects have 'sentimental value', not represented in any insurer's valuation, because they are invested with special associations. This capacity to invest possessions with qualities has played an important part in theorising about property, especially when the qualities invested are thought to relate to the person creating the object. The second aspect of the experience is the sense of invasion. Persons who have been robbed experience a violation of privacy; the person and the property constitute a sphere such that interference with the property is taken as interference with the person, and leads to a sense of personal violation or defilement. Hence it is not uncommon for people who have been burgled to move home, claiming that they could never again feel at ease in surroundings which had been 'invaded'. The detective who investigated the theft of the present writer's car had once had his own stolen. When it was recovered, he changed the steering-wheel and the gear knob, not liking to think that the thief had touched them.

This sort of experience is instructive; it serves to introduce the relation between property and personality in political theory. We shall see later that this takes many forms. Some have held that, in the act of production, an individual puts something of himself into the object, so that a special connection exists between producer and artifact. Others have thought that the type of property a person has, or the uses to which he puts it, are vital clues about his personality, or even his political capacity. Still others have held that particular personalities are associated with particular types of property, which are differentially desirable with respect to political organisation and political participation.

Although particular individuals may find that they are less inclined to take property for granted as a result of disappointed expectations or robbery, a more general (and less traumatic) challenge to an unreflective view is provided by exposure to social theory. This arises in two ways. First, in relation to 'property' as much as to other concepts which are central to social life, political theory has an indispensable role in showing that what seemed obvious, or capable of being taken for granted, is not in fact straightforward. Once we move beyond the level of extreme generality, it is not easy to elucidate the concept of property, any more than, for example, the concept of justice. 'Property defines mine and yours' does not get us very far, any more than 'justice is giving each his due'. Both may be true, but each needs elaboration before it provides any illumination. In the two cases, elaboration reveals that the same general notion may be understood in a number of more specific ways.

The second way in which social theory challenges the unreflecting view is by providing an historical dimension to the discussion. We have already seen that one anthropologist felt the need to stand aside from the prevalent concept of property she found in her own society, in order to develop a notion of more general application to the societies she and her colleagues were studying. Historical awareness not only leads to an interest in the origins of modern ideas, but also provides alternative perspectives which may help us not to take too much for granted. For example, many of today's readers are surprised to discover that Hobbes included 'conjugal affection' as a form of property, perhaps forgetting the parallel between 'to have and to hold', used in the marriage ceremony, and the same phrase used when referring to land tenure. Again, for many years, in England at least, a lawyer asked to give an account of the law of property would immediately assume that the question concerned land. It is obvious that what is regarded as 'property' has varied historically, and this helps to make us aware of the contingent nature of our present understanding.

A much more general point follows from such an awareness. Property institutions are fundamental to social life, whatever form they take. Their bedrock character helps to explain why they are often, at any one time, taken for granted. Nevertheless, almost everyone who has thought about politics seriously has something to say about property. Property provides links between an economic system, a legal system, and a political system. To say this does not presuppose that neat boundaries can be put round the 'systems' in question; property itself makes those boundaries ill-defined. At the same time, property has been seen as one way in which the boundaries between individuals are themselves delimited. The richness of the discussion of property in political theory, and the history of social thought, arises from the manifold ways in which it has been related to these 'systems'. Since there is nothing static about economic, political or legal organisation, a common attitude to the desirability of a particular form of property need not indicate any consensus in the reasons given.

Any discussion of property as an issue in political theory, then, must take account of both the conceptual problems involved, and the historical dimension of discussion. At the same time, of course, it must focus on issues of contemporary relevance. For these reasons, the present analysis begins with an exploration of the concepts of property and ownership, arguing that we should not understand 'property' in such a way as to exclude alternative contemporary meanings or historical usages. We need, in other words, a characterisation of property which embraces public, common and private variants, and which may be applied as readily to Hobbes's usage as to the practices of the societies which Hirschon and her collaborators studied. The elements of such a characterisation are specified in Chapter 3, as a prelude to a discussion of the debate about the origins of modern ideas. A selective review of some attempts to identify the 'history' of property, and to draw conclusions from that history, then allows us to identify a number of themes in those treatments, themes which are of abiding concern and certainly of importance today. These are the relations between property, liberty and power, discussed in Chapter 4; and between property and labour, explored in Chapter 5. Various problems posed by the role of property in linking resources to individuals through time are analysed in Chapter 6, before we conclude with a characterisation of the nature of the issues surrounding property in political theory. To avoid the charge that we brought against McCulloch, however, we begin with an exploration of the conceptual problems.

2 'Property', 'Ownership' and Political Theory

One initial difficulty in any attempt to impose some order on disputes about property in political theory arises from the delimitation of political theory itself. Broadly, theoretical considerations can be explanatory or justificatory. For example, a theory of property which held that the distribution of power in society was a product of the distribution of property in it would usually be attempting to explain how property has this effect, as well as claiming that it was present. Of course, such a theory would face conceptual difficulties: for example, it would have to elucidate the notion of power with which it was operating. On the other hand, a normative theory of property sets out to justify a particular set of arrangements governing property, or to show that an existing structure is defective with respect to some normative commitment. Such a theory discusses the legitimacy of property or tries to show how the identified deficiencies could be avoided. Obviously, this sort of theory also faces conceptual problems: the values it discusses need exploration, elucidation and defence. Explanatory and normative theories about property both need to consider what property is, and normative theories have to discuss what it should be or why the existing arrangements are defective.

The focus of explanatory and normative discussion, however, varies according to the sort of enquiry on which a writer is engaged. For example, as we shall shortly see, lawyers and economists understand property differently from each other. Although there is no harm in different understandings of a concept if everyone knows that various meanings are being attached to one term for different purposes, the situation can cause confusion. Political theory has always been an eclectic pursuit. It has characteristic concerns but is inevitably and necessarily informed by adjacent disciplines like law,

9

history, economics, sociology and philosophy. It is also informed by its own history: its characteristic concerns are, to some extent, timeless, even if historical contingency shapes particular responses. We might suggest, then, that putting boundaries round the political theory of property poses special difficulties, because property as a social institution is a legal, economic and political phenomenon and because political theory is itself eclectic. To limit ourselves to explicitly normative issues would be to exclude a large amount of discussion of characteristic concerns. For example, the theory that the distribution of power always and everywhere is a consequence of the distribution of property is both an historical and an empirical claim.

It is the eclectic nature of political theory which obliges us to ensure that we are not misled by the different notions of property found in the many obviously relevant discussions of the subject. To illustrate this point, the present chapter begins by looking at a number of studies in which the concept of property is employed. It is by no means intended to provide a survey of the literature, and it makes no claim to be exhaustive or comprehensive.

Ordinary language analysis

Frank Snare's article, 'The Concept of Property' (1972), sets out to tell us what is involved in the ordinary language meaning of property. Ordinary language is not quite common usage; it refers rather to careful speech, and analysis of it tries to bring out the complexity of distinctions embodied in usage. What is examined here is the way in which language-users think about property, and this leaves aside the technicalities and refinements which, say, a lawyer would find it necessary to introduce.

Snare claims that in ordinary language 'property' and 'ownership' are interchangeable terms. He says that he is indifferent as to whether the concept he elucidates is labelled by one or the other name. This claim applies to the way in which the terms are used now, and even if true should not lead us to suppose that ownership and property have always been used interchangeably. But Snare is correct to point out that in many cases a contemporary statement about ownership can be translated into a statement about property, and *vice versa*, without confusion. 'I own that car' and 'that car is my property' will usually convey the same information.

According to this account, ownership is defined by reference to a set of constituting rules. To say '*A* owns *P*' means that:

1. *A* has a right to use *P*.
2. Others may use *P* if, and only if, *A* consents.
3. *A* may permanently transfer the rights under rules 1 and 2 to specific other persons by consent.

In addition to these central rules, three others help to give meaning to ownership:

4. Punishment Rules, specifying what may happen to someone who either interferes with *A*'s use or himself wrongfully uses *P*.
5. Damage Rules, specifying that *B* may be required to pay compensation if he damages *P* without *A*'s consent.
6. Liability Rules, specifying that *A* may be held responsible if *P* causes certain sorts of damage. (Snare, 1972, pp.202–4)

The first point to note about this exposition is that, in common with any general account of ownership, it must rely on some idea of a usual case. For example, the right to use *P* is made central to this account. But the extent of possible use, of permissible use and of prohibited use vary as among types of property. The uses to which a house and a car may be put are quite different; and although this appears trivial, it points to the important aspect of indeterminacy that exists in ownership.

Owners may use their property in any way which is not prohibited, and since these possible uses are really limited only by imagination and inclination, it is not possible to list the permitted uses. This might suggest that we should therefore list the prohibited ones – but here again we shall run into trouble, because some prohibitions are general, and some are specific. That is, we shall need to know what *P* is (a teddy bear, a pet alligator, a dagger) before we can specify what uses are not permitted. Limitations on use are not insignificant. For example, under planning laws, zoning regulations and so on, the use of property may be quite strictly controlled.

Rule 2 is necessary because rule 1 makes no specification about exclusiveness. I have a right to the use of the public highway, and so does everyone else. This does not mean that persons who have such a right of use are entitled to exclude anyone else. In the case of private property, such an exclusion is nowadays usually understood; the right of use is exclusive to the owner. But because of the multiplicity of uses to which most property can be put, '*A* has a right to use *P* and to exclude others from its use without his permission' is not always correct. For example, a farmer may use his field to keep sheep. No doubt he is entitled to stop me keeping sheep on his land too, but he may not be able to prohibit me from walking across his field (to climb a hill, say, or just to admire the view), because the laws of trespass do not prohibit my presence on his land. My use, as in this example, may not produce any ill-effect. While the owner can prevent his property being used by others in some ways, he cannot always prevent them from using it at all.

It might be objected that these points about Snare's argument introduce legal detail into an account which is avowedly non-technical. But as we can see clearly from Rules 4–6, property is necessarily tied up with legalistic considerations of liability and responsibility. This raises the question of what the ordinary language conception of property is a conception of: what property is, under a set of legal rules, or what it should be, or what it is misconceived to be, where the legal rules are not wholly known or understood? In short, there is a danger that in looking at the ordinary language usage of property we are simply looking at an unreflective notion. In linguistic analysis a distinction between ordinary language use and a reconstructionist specification of a concept has been introduced. It has been argued that the ordinary understanding of, say, liberty, can be improved upon, in the sense that by specifiable criteria (for example, of discrimination, coherence, simplicity) a formation suggested by the analyst is better than that current amongst language users (e.g. Oppenheim, 1981, pp.1–2). In the case of property, there are standards which are not available in a case like liberty: we can ask whether the formulation gives us an accurate guide to property in a legal system, or how it compares with a more technical account. This does not mean that we expect every language-user to be a jurisprudent, any more than we would expect the same answer about the concept of energy from a physicist and a man in the pub.

Jurisprudence

Whether or not a person's interest in something is treated as property sometimes has definite legal consequences. For example, the Constitution of the United States of America provides protection of property against certain sorts of legislative and executive action. If an interest such as job security is treated as a person's property, then it will fall within this constitutional protection. As a consequence, someone might expect the law itself to define 'ownership'. But this is, unfortunately, not true. In the case both of 'property' and of 'ownership' the law does not often itself address the problem of 'what is property?' or 'what is ownership?' By and large, lawyers are interested in problems about who may legitimately do what and to whom: in what circumstances is someone guilty of a criminal offence, or in what circumstances is someone liable in a civil action? Answering these questions does not necessarily require an answer to the question, 'what is property?' or 'what is ownership?' For example, suppose that I take a lease of a flat in a house. A question may arise as to who is financially responsible for repairs. It is perfectly possible that the dispute will be resolved by reference to the 'freeholder' and 'leaseholder', without any mention of ownership or the owner at all. A further point follows from this: to elucidate the legal concept of ownership is not to explain a concept internal to the law in layman's language, as for example a physicist might explain the concept of energy in physics. It is, rather, to work out what is involved in the idea of ownership from the practice of lawyers. Obviously, if, in many cases, lawyers do not need to refer to ownership, then working out what constitutes ownership is in a sense a work of construction.

We must distinguish between 'ownership' and the presence of an owner. We may be able to list the rights and obligations which we think are contained within the concept of ownership, but if these rights and obligations are divided up among several persons we will not necessarily be able to identify an owner. This has been especially true if property is in the earth. The classic example of such a difficulty arises from the distinction between a freeholder and a leaseholder who has a long lease. Suppose I, as the freeholder, grant you a lease of 999 years on my house. One way of looking at the situation is to say that you and I are both owners: I own a freehold and you own a lease. But since the lease gives you rights of use, possession and management of the house for such an extended period, the object of my ownership is in effect a legal title to take the house back after 999 years. If we have to decide whom to call the owner, conventional wisdom holds that the reversioner is so treated. It is in one sense easier, however, to suppose that the reversioner and the leaseholder between them have the rights and obligations of ownership, so there is no single owner. Alternatively, we can either dispense with talk of the owner, which is what lawyers usually do, since for most purposes it is not necessary, or recognise two owners, the objects of whose ownership are conceptually separate.

In the case of this particular example, the difficulty arises from the history of the law of real property, and ultimately from the way in which the common law governing estates meshed with feudal ideas. These historical considerations play an important part in the development of ideas about ownership in law: as we shall see later, it has been argued that 'the' modern idea of ownership emerged in England, at least, in the seventeenth century, and part of the evidence for that thesis concerns new powers given to persons holding various sorts of estates in land.

'Ownership' is a very abstract notion, and to give an account of its content requires us to imagine a straightforward case, recognising that there will be exceptions and hazy areas. Even high-practised jurisprudents tend to talk about umbrellas, socks and toothbrushes when considering property. If we want to talk about the concept of ownership, we have to abstract from the details by imagining a simple case. This does not mean, however, that we should ignore aspects of ownership which lie beyond the analysis of it in law. To suggest an analogy: the examination of the constitution of a state does not often reveal who actually has power in it. Similarly, the discussion of the legal concept of ownership does not tell us whether ownership of the means of production confers power on the owners.

A very helpful analysis of ownership has been provided by A. M. Honoré (1961). He makes it clear that he is talking about the standard case of ownership as recognised by a mature legal system. His claim is that there are some things (umbrellas!) which are capable of being owned in the same way in all mature legal systems (p.108). The category of things owned in this way may be greater or smaller in various systems: for example, some societies do not recognise private property in the means of production. Honoré's claim is that all mature legal systems recognise ownership (as he describes it) in some things, not that all societies recognise it in all things or even in the same things. He calls the particular concept the 'liberal' concept of ownership.

Various questions arise here. First, how is ownership related to property? Secondly, why is this the 'liberal' concept of ownership? Thirdly, what is a mature legal system? We might also ask, if there are several concepts of ownership, of which the liberal concept is one variant, what are the others?

According to Honoré, the concept of ownership is closely related to the idea of the thing owned, and he suggests that 'property' is sometimes used 'to designate both' (p.128). Since 'property' refers sometimes to the legal relation, and sometimes to the thing which is the object of the relation, it follows that in one of its senses it is equivalent to ownership. Wesley Newcomb Hohfeld, author of a pathbreaking book on legal notions, made a similar point:

'Both with lawyers and with laymen this term [property] has no definite or stable connotation. Sometimes it is employed to indicate the physical object to which various legal rights, privileges, etc., relate; then again – with far greater discrimination and accuracy – the word is used to denote the legal interest (or aggregate of legal relations) appertaining to such a physical object.' (1919, p.28)

If 'the aggregate of legal relations' which Hohfeld mentions is the same as the set Honoré elucidates, then property in one of its senses is equivalent to ownership. We must also consider the case, however, in which the legal interest is not identical to that specified by Honoré. There may be an important difference here between ordinary language and legal usage. Snare's claim that property and ownership are interchangeable in ordinary talk does not entail that they are interchangeable in legal thinking, even if they are synonyms in a special case.

One distinction used in this context is that between rights *in rem* and rights *in personam*. Rights *in rem* and *in personam* are respectively rights conceived primarily as existing because of a relation between a person and a thing, and rights conceived primarily as existing because of a relation between persons. Obviously, all rights refer to relations between persons. The

distinction lawyers have in mind is often illustrated by contrasting
the result of my owning something with the result of my making a
contract with another person. In the first case, taken simply,
everyone else has to respect my ownership. In the second case, the
only person I can enforce my claims against is the other contractor.
Although my rights in both cases are rights against other persons,
the rights arise in the first case because of my legal relations with a
thing (my property) and in the second because of my legal relation
with a person (the other contractor). It soon appears, however, that
the distinction can be broken down, and different notions of
property reflect different judgements about the extent to which
rights *in personam*, at least in some cases, reproduce the features of
rights *in rem* (Dias, 1976, pp.396–406, esp. p.399n.3).

The relation between 'property' and 'ownership' is more
complicated in legal usage then it is in ordinary language, as
analysed by Snare. For him, ownership and property are
interchangeable. Honoré points out that ownership is equivalent to
property in *one* of its senses. Dias, listing meanings of property,
confirms this judgment, showing that 'property' can refer to things,
both physical and incorporeal, and to legal relations; and that the
sorts of legal relations it encompasses is a matter over which
analysts disagree.

The second question we put forward was: why does Honoré call
the concept of ownership he describes the 'liberal' one? We may
make two points which will have to be pursued in greater depth later
on. The first is that the general character of rights over property is
that they bestow on individuals the power to decide what should
happen to particular resources or 'things'; for example, in the case
of the ubiquitous umbrella, the owner can decide when to use it and
can exclude others from its use without permission. We met these
simple points in Snare's account of property. Inasmuch as
ownership confers rights, it confers a sort of freedom. On one view
of rights, their central logical characteristic is that they distribute
freedom between individuals. Property rights share this
characteristic, and to the extent that ownership of the kind
described by Honoré embraces such rights, it accords freedom to
individual owners. The 'liberal' concept of ownership, then, is one
which is concerned with the freedom of individual owners.

The second point to be made here also concerns the distribution
of freedom. There are two aspects to consider: the freedom of one

owner *vis-à-vis* another, and the freedom of an owner or owners *vis-à-vis* everyone else. An example of the first aspect arises from the power to bequeath property. If I am allowed to dispose of my property in such a way that I can effectively decide who shall enjoy it for the next (say) two hundred years, I am enjoying a power as part of my ownership which will be denied to subsequent 'owners'. Here the balance of freedom between two property owners in different generations will be unequal. An example of the second aspect arises when we consider what limits we want to place on the owner's capacity to decide on the use of his property. Not surprisingly, different liberal thinkers have filled in the content rather differently, depending upon their historical experience. When we come to look in more detail at the specification provided by Honoré, we shall see that certain elements of it 'balance' freedom between persons.

Our third initial question to put to Honoré was: what is a mature legal system? His claim is that *all* mature legal systems recognise liberal ownership in at least some things, and to assess this claim we need to know what a mature legal system is. It appears not to be merely contemporary systems, although most of Honoré's examples come from modern English, French, German and Soviet law. It would be difficult to deny that the Roman legal system was a mature one, and indeed Honoré draws comparisons with it. The absence of any criteria for the recognition of such mature systems, however, makes the assessment of Honoré's claim difficult.

Our final query concerned the number and designation of other concepts of ownership from which the liberal variant is to be distinguished. This point is related to our preceding concern, for some writers have argued that ideas about ownership have evolved over time, and they would therefore contrast an early notion with a medieval one and subsequently with a modern one. Honoré apparently has two contrasts in mind: that between a mature legal system and a 'primitive' one, and that between a liberal and a socialist regime, but since he argues that the liberal concept is to be found to some extent in all mature systems we are left unclear as to whether primitive systems or non-liberal regimes have rival concepts, or whether they simply truncate the application of the liberal concept.

Having glanced at these difficulties, let us look at Honoré's account in greater detail. Ownership is defined as '*the greatest*

possible interest in a thing which a mature system of law recognizes'
(p.108). The term which is immediately striking is 'greatest interest'
which suggests that interests in a thing can be arranged along some
dimension which measures their extent. 'Thing', in this context, as
we have seen already, has a broad application – it does not mean
simply physical items. 'The greatest interest' has two attractions as a
device to capture the ideas contained within 'ownership'. First, it
enables us to avoid talking about absolutes. It suggests not that
there is a set of specifiable powers, rights, liberties and obligations
which, when all present, constitutes ownership, but, rather, that
ownership can still exist when the set is not complete (a particular
right has been transferred) or when there are limits placed upon the
operation of particular rights or liberties. This is a complex point
which will be explained further shortly. The second attraction of
'the greatest interest' follows from the indeterminacy we noticed
earlier: it is not possible to specify all the actual or possible
limitations placed upon owners, yet the owner is, subject to those
limitations, able to do as he likes with his own. 'The greatest
possible interest' is then a device to describe the situation in which
ownership allows decisions to be made about the use (etc.) of a
thing, subject to limitations, without specifying all the possible uses
or the actual or possible limitations. Any limitation makes talk of
absolute ownership misleading; 'the greatest possible interest'
recognises this, while avoiding the difficulty of listing in great detail
the permitted or prohibited activities associated with ownership.

The idea of absolute ownership is therefore to be distinguished
from that of liberal ownership. 'Absolute ownership' has entered
the discussion largely because the term was thought at one time to
capture the practice of Roman law. It is now denied by some that
absolute ownership is adequate even as a description of that
(Lawson, 1958, p.57; Dias, 1976, p.406). Absolute ownership may
refer to the completeness (or perfection or indisputability) of title;
to the lack of restriction on use and enjoyment (restrictions may
arise because others have rights of use or enjoyment, or,
presumably, because no-one does); and to unlimited duration of
ownership. Of these senses, it is most difficult to imagine a system of
law which places no restrictions *whatever* on rights of use, and for
this reason it is sometimes denied that absolute ownership has ever
been recognised by or embodied in a legal system (Lawson, 1958,
p.6).

'Absolute ownership', then, is a conceptual device which enables us to imagine someone who has a perfect title to a thing, who can do as he likes with it, without sharing it unless he wishes, and who can transfer these rights to someone else, since ownership has no temporal limit. In practical cases, it is the second condition which is not met, since the law places all sorts of restrictions on use: even a car-horn may often not be used in a built-up area at night.

The fact that there is no absolute ownership, however, does not imply that there is no ownership. This is the attraction of talking about the greatest interest. One says, in effect, that although restrictions on use (etc.) are recognised, ownership entitles those in the proper legal relation to a thing to do much more than anyone else may legitimately do with respect to that thing. This is, then, how 'the greatest interest' avoids the problems of 'absolute ownership' and of indeterminacy.

In particular cases, nevertheless, there may well be a problem in deciding who has the 'greatest' interest. Here we must recall two points made earlier about the analysis of ownership. First, elucidating the content of 'ownership' does not entail that 'there is always an owner'. Second, whether the 'right of ownership' exists independently of the rights and liabilities which constitute ownership is disputed. These points are related in the following way. If I own a car, and I lend it to you for a period (say a week), we do not think that my ownership has ceased, even though I cannot myself use the car during that period. One way of looking at the situation is to say that I can give away or transfer various rights (and liabilities) which are part of the content of ownership, and yet retain the right of ownership. Another view, however, is that 'ownership' simply *is* the rights and liabilities in question. On this view, these rights and liabilities may become so dispersed that there is no one 'owner'; it would still be true that the rights and liabilities constitute ownership, and that if they all came into the same person's hands that person would be owner.

What are these rights and liabilities which constitute the content of 'ownership'? Honoré lists the following incidents: the rights of use, of management, to possess, to an income, to security, to capital; transmissibility; absence of term; prohibition of harmful use; liability to execution; and residuary character. The most obvious point will now be familiar: ownership carries with it liabilities and obligations. Some of these liabilities and obligations reflect the rights of other owners, but more generally ownership is regulated by many different principles. Hence Honoré includes the prohibition of harmful use as an incident of ownership although it is true that the harmful uses to which an air-rifle and a pocket comb may be put will differ. It is also true, of course, that the prohibition of harmful use does not entail that the owner will be forbidden to, much less prevented from, imposing burdens on others. One characteristic of rights is that they regulate the extent to which such burdens may legitimately be imposed on others (Flathman, 1976). 'Harmful use' is not *any* use by which someone may feel disbenefitted, for ultimately all uses might be cast in that light, but only such uses as are discountenanced by law with aims such as the prevention of assault.

The rights listed are straightforward, but it is worth noticing that the way in which they are formulated deliberately takes into account the practices of modern commercial life. The right to the capital is, in effect, the right to sell the thing, and it is described as the right to the capital partly to distinguish it from the right to an income and the right to manage the thing, which may be separately exercised, sometimes by persons employed for the purpose or by persons who pay a fee to acquire those rights. Since the use of a thing can (often) be sold separately from the thing itself (for example, a local firm offers to hire to me or to sell to me a cement-mixer), it is worth distinguishing between transferring a right for value and transferring ownership altogether. As we shall see, this is an important consideration in the economists' approach to property. It is another reflection of the fact that persons can transfer part of their interest in a thing without losing the rest of their interest.

The other incidents (apart from the prohibition of harmful use, and the rights) need more explanation. They represent Honoré's attempt to capture the practice of law: they try to cover the points about the nature of ownership which we discussed earlier. 'Residuary character' taken together with 'absence of term', covers the case where part of an interest is transferred, and yet reverts to the transferror after a time. For example, if I borrow a cement-mixer from the local tool hire company, I have the use of it for the hire period. At the end of that period, I have either to pay more money to extend the hire, or to return the mixer. The hire company is denying itself a right of use for a period, but reacquiring it at the end of the period. So ownership contains this 'reverting' – when an interest temporarily granted expires, it reverts to the owner. 'Absence of term' is closely related, because many lesser interests expire at particular times, while ownership has no temporal limit. A particular owner can bring *his* ownership to an end, but what he transfers or gives up is an interest not limited in time. It is at this point that we can see the difficulty described earlier about separating 'parts' of ownership. Very often, it seems natural to say that the person who acquires an interest from another comes to own something himself: for example, a freeholder grants a long lease, and it seems natural to think of the lessee as owning something; he can use and manage the property, perhaps sublet it to provide an income, or sell the lease entirely. Because of the imprecision of 'things', the object of ownership, such interests are often treated as bringing into existence something capable of being owned. So when ownership is apparently divided, as between the freeholder and the lessee, we may find that both are treated as owners, but of different things. As Lawson puts it, 'This puzzling English habit adds appreciably to the difficulty which the student experiences in studying property law' (1958, p.9).

Transmissibility is concerned with the present holder's ability to pass on his interest at death: his property may be transmitted to his heirs. It is important to notice that such a transmission could operate by law – that is, all property which a person owned would, at his death, become the property of his heirs, whatever the deceased wished. Or it could be transmitted to those whom he wished to benefit. In either case, it is part of ownership that it outlasts the present owner. The terms on which this transmission should be allowed, if at all, have been a central concern for political theorists, for obvious reasons, and we shall look at the issue in a later chapter.

Finally, liability to execution is Honoré's terminology to cover the situation where an owner may find his property taken away from him, for example, to pay his debts. This is one of the balancing considerations to which reference was made earlier, for if there is to be security of property some mechanism like execution may sometimes be necessary to provide it.

For the political thinker, perhaps, two other ways in which an owner can 'lose' his property are of greater significance. These are taxation and expropriation. Honoré does not include these as incidents of ownership because he thinks that this would obscure the difference between taxes on what is earned and taxes on what is owned, in the first case, and because he thinks expropriation falls on special sorts of property, in the second (pp.123–4). Liability to taxation may not be an incident of ownership, but political theory has been concerned with the relationship between security of property and the activities of the state. We have seen that one reason for thinking the concept of 'absolute ownership' unhelpful in modern times is that the state reckons to regulate property. The forms of this regulation will vary and the limits of permissible state regulation or interference will be set in different places; but no state denies itself such regulatory interference completely. The prohibition of harmful use is one variant of that interference; compulsory purchase is another; and the latter also puts limits on the completeness of 'the absence of term'. The proper limit of the state's activity in this respect is a central issue in political theory. The state is the law-making body, and there is no guarantee that present laws will be maintained, so there is a good case for considering liability to the state's activity in an assessment of ownership. A crisis like the outbreak of war, for example, may lead the state to make more insistent claims to resources.

We must now examine the idea of title, which we came across in the discussion of absolute ownership. It may have struck the reader that the content of ownership does not give a complete account of how it arises or ceases. The different ways of acquiring or parting with property are ways of acquiring or losing title. The usual ways in which title is acquired are transfer from a living person and succession to the property of a deceased person. It is clear that these mechanisms cannot fully explain the acquisition of title, because they both assume that title already rests somewhere. Obviously, then, we shall face an infinite regression until we find title to something being established. At this point, we are looking for ways in which property could legitimately be introduced – and there are many proposals on this score. We shall defer consideration of them to subsequent chapters.

We may conclude, then, that analysis of the concepts of property and ownership in law is not only difficult, but also, perhaps, surprisingly difficult. The surprise arises from the expectation that here we shall find a clear technical vocabulary, an expectation defeated by the fact that lawyers can often achieve their practical results without making much use of these concepts. The difficulty arises from the complexity of law – it has developed over time, and bears the imprint of its history. The major reason why a lot of practical business can be conducted without reference to ownership is ultimately itself historical: many actions to protect interests were developed before the modern (liberal?) notion of ownership (e.g. Simpson, 1961). This fact plays an important part in disputes about the history of the ideas of property and ownership, and consequently in the interpretation of political theory written in earlier centuries.

Economics

Economists have approached the notion of property from one special perspective, namely that there will be a causal connection between the set of 'property rights' which are enforceable in any society and its level of economic performance. A particularly good example of this approach may be found in the work of R. Posner. The function of property rights, he suggests, is to 'create incentives to use resources efficiently' (1973, p.10). Exclusive 'property rights' are a necessary but not sufficient condition of the efficient use of resources. Two points may be noticed. First, resources, the focal point of the analysis, are substituted for the 'things' which are the object of ownership in the legal analysis. We have already seen that 'things' is vaguely, if not arbitrarily, used in the legal analysis; but is 'resources' more specific? It is the simple starting point of most text books on economics that the subject matter of that discipline is the allocation of scarce resources. Resources are any object of want: something persons wish for either because it provides direct satisfaction of wants or needs (such as water wanted by a thirsty man) or because it provides for the indirect satisfaction of those wants and needs (such as a well). But since allocation becomes a problem only when resources do not match needs and wants, property rights should perhaps be conceived of not so much as a mechanism which provides for the efficient use of resources *as such*, but as one which provides for the efficient use of *scarce* resources.

The second point which will be noticed about the functional account of property rights is that they contribute towards 'efficiency'. 'Efficiency' is a notion with descriptive and prescriptive implications. Posner himself stresses three characteristics of an 'efficient' set of property rights: it is universal, in the sense that all resources are either owned, or capable of being owned, by someone; it is exclusive, in the sense that other persons may be excluded from enjoyment of the object of the property right; and the 'property rights' are themselves transferable (Posner, pp.11–13). Now clearly this analysis does not claim that *all* property rights in the world have the function of promoting efficiency. So what is at stake is a recommendation: if you wish to promote efficiency, structure property rights to achieve that result. To accept this recommendation, we should need to be committed to 'efficiency', so we are entitled to ask what that involves (Baker, 1975).

We should notice that both property rights and ownership are used in the context of this sort of analysis in a different way to those we have already encountered. First, 'property rights' are very widely interpreted. We can do no better than to quote Demsetz, in many ways the founding father of this approach: 'when a transaction is concluded in the market place, two bundles of property rights are exchanged' (1967, p.347). It will be clear that the crude distinction between property and contract which separates rights *in personam* from rights *in rem* is ignored by this formulation. For example, if you contract with me to provide a plumbing service, and I agree to pay you, this is a transaction concluded in the market place. If the rights transferred are *property* rights, this can only be because I am conceived to have acquired some sort of property in your labour, or the product of your labour, and you are conceived to have acquired a property claim on my money. A lawyer would find this puzzling, however, because he would think simply of the rights and obligations arising from the contract, which seem to have nothing to do with property. Because it is allegedly a requirement of an efficient system of property rights that they be transferrable, it seems that all transactions are treated as transferring property rights. A corollary of this is that economists talk about ownership as a bundle of property rights; but ownership, in jurisprudence, is considered to carry liabilities with it.

Obviously different usages are legitimate provided no confusion results. The economists' stress on the relation between property rights and efficiency makes transferability central, and this is primarily a matter of exchange and sale for value. But many aspects of what persons find important about property are of course not connected with exchangeability, or market value. 'Sentimental value' and security, stability and personalised space do not rest on market value (although market value may, of course, be affected by changes in security). Pryor's insistence that property rights must have an *economic* value narrows the focus: 'Property is a bundle of rights or set of relations between people with regard to some good, service or "thing"; such rights must have economic value and must be enforced in some societally recognised manner' (1973, p.375).

That something has value, and that it is exchangeable, are two distinct requirements. One of the best examples of this is provided by pension funds, which undoubtedly have a value to persons who have claims upon them. Nevertheless, pension rights (claims) are not usually transferable: the value they possess cannot be realised except by drawing the pension. Conversely, many things are exchangeable (in the sense that it is permissible to exchange them or give them away) which will nevertheless not realise any market value. Market value is a matter of the price something will fetch; economic value may exist where there is not market value. That something is exchangeable is a necessary but not a sufficient condition of its having market value, and neither necessary nor sufficient for it to have economic value. So Posner's condition of an efficient set of property rights (that they be transferable) and Pryor's condition (that they have economic value) will give different sets of 'property'.

Consider the position of the heir of an entailed estate. The law will operate to give this person the land when the present holder dies. The presumptive 'heir' has a reasonable expectation of an inheritance, and he may certainly be able to borrow against this expectation. His interest certainly has an economic value. But it does not have a market value in the sense that he can sell it: he can sell neither the right to inherit nor the land itself. Here, then, the land is transferable (by succession) and the heir's interest has an economic value, but he cannot sell it (and therefore it has no market value).

As well as universality and exclusivity which the approach seems to require, the conditions are *both* that rights are alienable and that they possess value. The unifying theme in the economic approach to property rights is that the costs and benefits of a person's activities should rebound on him (as far as possible), and only on him (as far as possible). Property rights are to be structured (if necessary, re-structured) so that the harmful or beneficial effects of a person's activities are brought to bear on him rather than other people. If there were a property right in clean air, smokers would have to buy the right to smoke. This would convert the disbenefits experienced by others into a cost to the smoker, and non-smokers could decide how much money they would need to receive to compensate for the smoke. Similarly, if there were a right to smoke, non-smokers could pay smokers to desist. These solutions require both property rights and a market (Coase, 1960).

The economic approach to property rights, then, aims to specify the set of such rights which provides the greatest incentive to use resources efficiently. We should notice that it rests on a different view of property and ownership from that of the lawyers. Before accepting its recommendations about the desirable structure of property rights, we should need to accept all the assumptions about the relationship between efficiency and welfare on which it rests, and all the behavioural assumptions which are built into it. From one perspective, production and distribution are both dependent on the structure of property rights. We shall explore two other aspects of this relation in subsequent chapters – the thesis that 'the modern' idea of property has emerged with a particular capitalist or commercial society, and that a clear relationship exists between property and economic or political power.

Economic and legal history

The same relationship between 'property rights' and efficiency provides the basis for North and Thomas's study, *The Rise of the Western World* (1973), in which they relate different rates of economic growth to different sets of property rights. Changes in property rights are largely accounted for by seeing them as 'rational', since they go further to reduce the discrepancy between individual activity and the social costs and benefits of it. The study has been criticised for giving insufficient attention to power in its account of the changes in property rights.

A similar problem arises in legal history. It is widely accepted that the law of contract was radically altered in late seventeenth-century England, even though the details are a matter of debate. Describing such changes is often difficult enough: explaining them raises additional problems. A great deal of legal history stresses considerations internal to the law, such as the acceptability of particular arguments to judges. Combining a story about economic rationality with the detail of legal change and with a realistic assessment of the distribution and use of power in explaining changes is very hard.

There is, in addition, a conceptual problem. When we encountered Honoré's exposition of 'ownership', we noticed that he was concerned with the 'liberal' concept, and that it was uncertain to what extent this designation was restricted to present-day legal systems. It is clear that historically the 'liberal' concept may not always have been present. The question then arises as to what other concepts of ownership have existed, and how we would identify them. Alternatively, we may feel that before the emergence of the liberal idea there was no notion of ownership. To be sure, there may have been rights related to property: but we have seen that this is compatible with the absence of ownership as now understood. In short, the idea of ownership has a history, and we need to look at whether there are different concepts of ownership or one concept which emerges at an identifiable time.

A similar point may be made about 'property'. Apart from movements between common property and private property (for example, the conversion of common land into private property during the enclosures), there are additions to, and deletions from, the list of 'things' which can count as property. For instance, other persons were considered 'things' in societies which practised slavery. A history of property would have to take this into account. But it also faces a problem of identifying different notions of property appropriate to the balance between private and common and to the list of items which may be property. We shall pursue these points in the next chapter, which deals with evolutionary accounts of property and the history of ownership.

Normative analysis

Normative analysis of property is concerned with the relationship between property and values like liberty and justice. It explores how such a social institution should be structured. Obviously, writers have been concerned with the desirable structure of property rights and obligations for centuries: usually, what they have had to say about property has been embedded in a broad social philosophy which draws out their views on human nature and its consequences for social organisation. So justifications of desired property systems have usually been attached to a large range of assumptions and presuppositions.

In addition to this traditional concern, there has been a more particular focus on property within political theory in recent years. It has two main causes. First, C. B. Macpherson (1962) produced an interpretation of the political theory of the seventeenth century which laid great emphasis on the social assumptions under which authors like Hobbes and Locke were writing, and these social assumptions turned out to have an economic focus, in which property was very important. In the course of the disputes about interpretation which his thesis occasioned, scholars have been led to look closely at the attitudes to property, including its justification, which these writers evinced. Secondly, Robert Nozick (1974) produced a widely-read book in which he assumed the primacy of individual rights in general, and property rights in particular. His own theory's emphasis on the importance of property has been critically reviewed; and this too has led to discussion of the justifiability of private property (Paul, 1981). Partly in response to Nozick's discussion, Lawrence C. Becker (1977) wrote about the 'philosophic foundations' of property rights. He tried to classify the arguments for and against private property, and his book remains the only general analysis of justificatory arguments.

According to Becker, attempts to justify the institution of private property have been based upon 'the argument from first occupancy', the 'labour theory of property acquisition', various arguments from 'utility' or from 'political liberty' and from 'considerations of moral character'. Becker is concerned to discuss the adequacy of these attempts at justification, and to mention 'anti-property arguments' which dispute the justification of private property.

It will be clear that before we can discuss the adequacy of a justification, we need to know what it is that needs to be justified. The normative analysis therefore has as a precondition the sort of conceptual exploration on which we have been engaged. Becker suggests three levels of justification:

'A *general* justification of property rights gives an answer to the question of why there ought to be any property rights – of any sort – at all. A *specific* justification gives an answer to the question of why there ought to be a specific *sort* of property right (e.g. full, liberal ownership of land). A *particular* justification gives an answer to the question of why a particular person ought to have a particular property right in a particular thing.' (1977, p.23)

We might have some doubts about the possibilities of sorting out justificatory arguments in this way, however. First, it is difficult to imagine how a general justification could proceed until some particular or specific elements were introduced. We would need an argument for property rights which did not specify what sorts of rights they were and did not tell us who was to enjoy them. In other words, the apparent separability of these levels of justification may be illusory. Secondly, the level of specific justification is inspecific as to whether it is concerned with a sort of property right or a particular bundle of rights, liabilities and responsibilities. As we have seen, full liberal ownership is not a *sort* of property right; it is one way of aggregating rights and liabilities with respect to a thing. Thirdly, the particular justification is particularised in three ways which are more conveniently separated. It discusses particular persons, particular rights, and particular things. We may well find it more helpful to distinguish *who* may have property (for example, slaves were usually disbarred) from what things may be property (umbrellas, or the means of production) from particular rights (should there be a right to destroy property, or simply to use it?). This point may be pursued by looking at the idea of 'public ownership'.

Public property and public ownership

The 'liberal ownership' which we have been looking at up to now obviously relates to private property. The relation between private property and other property, or between individual ownership and other versions of ownership, is contested in two different ways. First, there is dispute about the historical pattern, or, if 'pattern' is too presumptive, about historical experience. Many writers have argued that some form of common or public property preceded the introduction of individual property, and some have gone on to organise a pattern in historical experience which places great stress on the development of property. Secondly, there is dispute about the extent to which it makes sense to talk of public property and public ownership (e.g. Arendt, 1958, pp.256–7).

Although the central contrast drawn is between private and public property or ownership, we should remember that property has been attributed to a large class of entities: the public, God, the state, the community, corporations and business firms, churches, charities, the family. Council houses are sometimes described as public property. Locke thought that God's creatures were his property: 'For Men being all the Workmanship of one Omnipotent, and infinitely wise Maker . . . sent into the World by his order and about his business, they are his Property, whose Workmanship they are . . .' (Locke, 1965, II, §6). In 'The Demands of the Communist Party in Germany', Marx and Engels announced: 'The estates of princes and other feudal lords, and all mines and pits, etc., shall become state property' (1973, p.109). In many parts of England there is still a common, which historically was land attached to a parish and used communally, and in Scotland some terraced houses still have common land attached to them. Business firms own property: beer crates, for example, marked 'property of Allied Breweries'. Finally, Bodin and other thinkers have held that property is a right of the family, not of individuals (Nisbet, 1976, p. 142). The public, then, is only one of a number of entities other than individuals to whom property or ownership has been attributed.

It is helpful to look at the range of these entities, for clearly some are more analogous to the individual case than others. Business firms, for example, may be treated as fictitious persons; that is, the law designates a unit which is clearly not an individual in such a way that it may be treated as if it were. If we treat Allied Breweries, for example, as a fictitious person, we can attribute powers, rights and responsibilities to it as we would to an individual. In this case, individual private ownership is the model for 'the property of Allied Breweries'.

Of course, the creation of a fictitious person, an enterprise in this example, still requires us to specify the links between real individuals – workers, managers, directors, shareholders – and the fictitious person. We need to know how decisions about Allied Breweries' property are taken, who is entitled to sue someone causing damage to the property and so on. Although there is certainly an analogy between individual property and a firm's property the special circumstances of enterprises will obviously lead to differences in the treatment of property.

One aspect of the connection between natural persons and fictitious persons which has been thought important in the analysis of enterprises is the so-called divorce of ownership from control (Parry, 1969, p.51). Those who are treated as owning Allied Breweries, namely the shareholders, are not in charge on a day-to-day basis. Those who are charged with acting for the company, the directors, obviously delegate much of the managerial function to professionals. Although we can treat an enterprise like a person, the close connection between ownership and control which is usually found when individuals are owners may not exist. This may be important in several ways: first, some defences of private property assume that property confers control, and secondly if control and ownership are not directly connected, some of the apparent difference between private and public ownership may evaporate. With the reservations given, then, we can see that the property of entities the law chooses to treat as persons may be treated as similar to individual property.

Our second example was Locke's attribution of property to God. This attribution is partly a matter of Locke's idea that a person who expends labour may generate a title to that with which his labour is mixed, or to the product of his labour. This argument will be examined in a later chapter. But the thought which underlies Locke's attribution relates both to 'workmanship', a consideration which we postpone, and to power, and it has a secular parallel. For Locke, each person has a property in his own person, while God has a property in everyone. So the property each has with respect to others is subject to the property which God has in all. The secular parallel is the claim of the state over the property of citizens. The state claims at least a regulatory interest in citizen's property. In some versions, for example the doctrine of eminent domain, the state has some sort of property interest. The parallel to Locke's view of God's property is obvious enough, but when the overarching power is the state we should be careful to distinguish

32   *Property*

the state's relation to citizens' property, and any claims it might
make on that account, from the state's ownership of property as
such.

'State ownership' and 'public ownership' are often used in ways
which suggest that the terms are interchangeable. The reason,
probably, is that one form of state ownership prevents the existence
of private property, and that public ownership is usually intended as
an antithesis to private ownership. We may take as an example of
the use of 'state' and 'public', in the context of ownership, the
following quotation from Hugh Gaitskell's essay, *Socialism and
Nationalisation*:

'[A distinction can be drawn between] *nationalisation*, which is
generally understood to mean the taking over by the State of a
complete industry so that it is owned by, and managed and
controlled for the community, and *public ownership*, which
strictly speaking means the ownership by the community of any
property, whether individual or not, whether embracing the
whole of an industry or only part of it.' (1956, p.6)

Gaitskell goes on to point out that the State's ownership of
commercial or industrial property need not involve detailed control
over any particular firm, even less a whole industry (1956, pp.34–6).

In this context it is worth looking more closely at the 'state', 'the
public' and 'the community', and at the connections between them.
The 'public' is an elusive unit, but talk of the public is generally
intended to refer to an inspecific group of persons. The membership
of the public is indeterminate (as against, say, members of a trade
union or political party). When someone describes a park as being
'public property', he is suggesting that an indeterminate group
enjoys rights of use over it. There are no special qualifications to be
met before access is permitted, although there may be rules
permitting exclusion, for example that persons are not allowed
access if drunk. A public park, then, is open to anyone prepared to
obey the rules governing its use. The contrast is between the
indeterminacy of 'anyone' and specific qualifications. A public
library is open to anyone (who is prepared to obey the rules, and
perhaps with a residence qualification) while a private library is
available only to the owner and those whom the owner chooses to

admit. In the first case, a right to use follows for anyone who fulfils general conditions; in the second, a right to use may be derived only from the owner.

In the case of public property, then, rights of use are available for the benefit of a group of persons. This does not mean, however, that the title to the property rests with them. Those who have a right to use a public park do not collectively own it. The title to the land normally rests with a local authority. Partly because the local authority is accountable to 'the public', and partly because the purpose of the ownership is to provide benefits to the public, such property is described as public. But the local authority could sell it on the land market. The case is similar with public transport. Anyone prepared to pay the fare is entitled to use it, but the public does not collectively own the rolling stock, in the way that the shareholders in Allied Breweries collectively own the assets of that company. Public property, then, is characterised by the separation of beneficial use, available to an indeterminate group, from title, which may be held by a body more or less immediately accountable to the public. 'Non-exclusion', of course, does not imply the absence of any price or other rationing mechanism. In fact, the generality of access may well make such rationing procedures more necessary. Libraries ration the number of books any particular individual may have on loan. Public seats go to the first arrivals. Public transport employs queues, price mechanisms and a first-comer allocation of particular seats. The difference between such systems and a private property system may sometimes appear marginal. Its locus is entitlement. Under a regime of private property, the owner has a general right to exclude others from the use of his property, but grants the right of use to others, normally in return for value received. In the case of public transport, the owner usually has a duty to make use available to the public, but may nevertheless make charges and employ rationing procedures to discriminate amongst those who might wish to take up the option.

It follows from what has already been said about public property that public ownership is often a misnomer. The title to public property may rest with a particular agency which is entitled to deal with it in the same way as any other owner. Nevertheless, such ownership may be enmeshed in a structure of accountability, so that the particular agency may be treated as a trustee for the public. Although the public is not collectively the owner, the agency in which title vests is supposed to control and dispose of the property in the interests of the public.

Many of the examples of public property we have discussed are concerned with local or municipal government. If we use public ownership to highlight the beneficiaries of ownership (*not* the holders of title), we should recognise that it exists at levels other than that of the state. Municipal ownership, state ownership and nationalisation could then be treated as forms of public ownership. The first two are distinguished by the location of title, while the third is a special case of the second.

Community property, or common property, need not be public property, despite Gaitskell's usage. For example, in many areas of Scotland a group of dwellings has a common green attached to it. Agreement between the owners (or inhabitants) of these dwellings governs acceptable use of the green. It is certainly *not* the case that the public has any rights over the ground, for the special qualification is living in one of the particular houses. Indeed, such greens are often surrounded by fences and locked gates to restrict access to those entitled to enjoy it. One form of common property, then, gives rights of use and enjoyment (and perhaps management) to a *specific* group of persons. Such common rights may exist irrespective of where the title to the land (in this example) is vested. The title to so-called common land in England often rested in the freeholder of the manor. It was 'common' only because those living in the manor had rights over it – usually rights to graze animals. A second form of common property exists where a group of persons collectively owns something – as shareholders collectively own a firm, or as husband and wife jointly own household possessions. Whether the community be the manor or the household, in these examples, it is certainly not the public. This has the important implication that while public property or public ownership may require the intervention of an agency or trustee, since 'the public' cannot exercise the rights (etc.) of an owner directly, common property may not. A smaller number of persons can act together. Even large companies have shareholders' meetings where *some* degree of exercise of ownership rights occurs.

There is one important difference between the example of manorial grazing rights and the example of the shareholders of a joint stock company. In the first case, each commoner has rights over the whole. In the second case, the shareholder owns part of the whole, and, of course, the ratio between part and whole is the ratio of the number of his shares to the total issued. Shareholders jointly own the firm; commoners each have property rights over the whole common. It is possible to combine the two models, but it is not necessary to do so.

Nationalisation, in Gaitskell's idea of it, is the ownership, management and control of a complete industry for the community. We have noted already that, in the case of private business firms, based on joint-stock models, a divorce between ownership and control has been postulated. Ownership is divided between the shareholders, who may be very numerous. The management of the company's day-to-day affairs rests with professionals. Many arguments about private property – whether favourable or antipathetic – suppose that ownership and control go hand in hand. Marx had noted that joint stock companies were a step towards the socialisation of ownership, or at least a step away from the simple model of the individual factory owner controlling his own workforce directly. Different versions of 'public ownership', including nationalisation, lead to different complexities about ownership and control.

Clearly, nationalised industries employ professional managers, just as private industry does. The managerial elite need be no less prominent in the one than the other. But there may in any case be no clear relationship between 'ownership' and control in cases of 'public ownership'. For example, the state until recently owned a majority of the shares in British Petroleum. Since BP is not a 'whole industry', the case on Gaitskell's definition would be of public ownership, which in this example would be merely the state's ownership of 51 per cent of the shares. Of course, this gives the state 'control' to the extent that such a share-holding can never be defeated in a vote. But the same level of control might in practice be achieved with a smaller share holding. If the state owned 40 per cent of the shares, and the other 60 per cent were held by individuals who had one share each, it is unlikely that effective control would be diminished.

To treat the BP case as an example of 'public ownership' not only makes public ownership compatible with (rather than opposed to) private ownership, but also makes the concept of public ownership dependent upon that of private ownership. That is, public ownership works in the same way as private ownership, and there is simply a difference in the agency which holds the property. A share in a company is property; the state has some shares; 'public' is substituted for 'the state', and the shares are said to be publicly owned. If the shareholding is large enough, it is said that the company is publicly owned. This is misleading for three reasons. First, it is the state and not the public which is the owner. Secondly, it is shares rather than the company which is owned. Thirdly, public ownership is usually advocated as the negation of private ownership, and no such negation here occurs.

Similar considerations to these have motivated two different complaints about the concept of public ownership. On the one hand, Hannah Arendt denied that it was a useful concept, because the public could not own anything in a way remotely analogous to a private individual. This point connects with the question raised above: is public ownership modelled on private ownership, or is it to be its negation? On the other hand, R. N. Berki has pointed out, in his essay on socialism, that 'public ownership' has been used to refer to a great variety of property arrangements and economic systems:

> ' "Public ownership" as a general formula is too indefinite, too indiscriminate to have any concrete meaning. It can refer to central planning with complete state ownership of resources; to the nationalization of large industrial and financial concerns only; to state shareholding in private enterprise; to co-determination; to public corporations; to decentralized economies; to workers' control; to producers' co-operatives; and so on and so forth.' (Berki, 1975, p.10)

Whilst we may note that some of these references seem more appropriate than others, it seems clear that when we are discussing property rules it is more helpful to specify the actual or desired arrangements in more detail than the vagueness of 'public ownership' allows. This is particularly important when recommendations for a particular property system follow from a critique of private property – for we wish to be clear in exactly what respect the proposed system will overcome the deficiences identified by the critique. For example, if there is an objection to private ownership of the means of production on the ground that it confers power on the owners, we should want to examine proposed alternatives to see what power structure might accompany them –

and here it would make a great difference whether, for example, state ownership of productive resources or collective (producers') ownership were envisaged.

A general account of property needs to embrace common property, private property and public property as variants. It should also pinpoint what may vary among concepts of property, and identify what we would need to know about a particular legal system to describe its treatment of property. Such a general account would also indicate what a justification of property needs to justify. In Chapter 3, we shall be primarily concerned with the normative implication of histories of property. But since such histories also require a treatment of property 'in general', we shall begin by providing a framework for property before examining the potential significance of disputes about its history. These historical themes will introduce the thematic treatments of Chapter 4, in which the connection between property (on one side) and liberty and power (on the other) is examined; of Chapter 5, which looks at the relationship between labour (broadly conceived) and property; and of Chapter 6, which discusses arguments about property located in time – whether, for example, inheritance should be allowed.

3 On the 'History' of Property

This chapter is concerned with the 'history' of property, and links the conceptual issues addressed in Chapter 2 with the themes of later discussions. The need for such a link arises because anyone concerned with the history of property needs to explain what it is, while any particular history of property will suggest connections between property and aspects of social life like the division of labour and political liberty. We shall be concerned, in this chapter, with problems which arise from the recognition that property is not invariable. There are three major problems of this kind. First, since 'property' may refer to both material resources and legal relations, to ideas and to concrete arrangements, how are these to be brought together in the historical account? Secondly, if property can take various forms, or be embodied in different property-systems, what general characteristics does it have? Finally, how have arguments about the history of property been conceived to affect the legitimacy of particular property institutions? It will be seen that these problems straddle the conceptual issues and the themes identified.

Paul Lafargue tells us that property 'is not immutable and always the same, but, on the contrary, it, like all material and intellectual phenomena, incessantly evolves and passes through a series of forms which differ, but are derived, from one another' (1975, p.3). Lafargue went on to provide an account of the way in which this phenomenon had, in his view, altered, and he called it *The Evolution of Property from Savagery to Civilisation*. Of course, not everyone would accept the assumptions upon which this history was written, but presumably few will deny Lafargue's initial proposition, that property 'is not immutable and always the same'.

Both ideas about property, and institutional arrangements

concerned with it, have, of course, changed over time. And co-existing societies have different understandings and practices. If we want to give an account of property which does not commit us to any particular variant of it – private property, say – we need a characterisation which covers the variants and yet is capable of exhibiting them as examples of the general case. Any attempt to write a history of property clearly faces the same problem. If we grant that property is an alterable social institution, we need an account of its characteristics so that particular historical variants can be exhibited as examples of that broad characterisation. The account of property 'in general' is reciprocally related to accounts of its particular forms, as identified by the theorist. The relation between the two influences discussion of the 'naturalness' of 'property' and ideas about possible property arrangements.

In the next section, a general account of 'property' is offered. It is formal, in the sense that it specifies no particular concept of property, only the ways in which concepts or practices differ. We shall then look at the ways in which various theorists have identified significant historical variations in property, and examine the normative uses to which they put their arguments. The variety of considerations brought to bear on determining the character of desirable property institutions will be introduced – instances are God's intentions, economic efficiency and social harmony – as a prelude to the thematic treatments of later chapters.

A framework for 'property'

Objects of property. Different lists of 'things' capable of being property would reflect very different kinds of social organisation, as is clear from the example of slavery. We have encountered Honoré's claim that ownership as he describes it extends to some things in all mature legal systems. If we were interested in comparing two such systems, we should want to know *which* things. If we found the means of production on one list but not another, we would obviously expect other variations between the societies. To anticipate another item in this catalogue, we should also want to know about objects of property which could be the property only of particular persons – as mining rights are the property of the Coal Board.

Means of acquisition, transfer and loss. We saw that knowing the content of ownership does not tell us how it arises or comes to an end for a particular property holder. 'Acquisition' here refers both to acquisition by a different person of something which is already another's property, and to original acquisition. We need to know about both to avoid the infinite regress mentioned earlier. Under this heading, then, we would cover 'title' in the legal discussion, and also the normative arguments about how a system of property could justifiably arise. Transfer of property can take place both *inter vivos* and at death. We would want to know how property is transferred between the living, and about inheritance institutions. For example, if succession to land is by operation of law rather than by the will of the deceased, the relationship between family and property would be significantly different.

The status of particular persons or groups of persons. An exploration of property needs to pay attention not only to what may be property, but also to who may hold it. Discrimination between persons with respect to who may hold property is clearly something which needs justification, as much as the inclusion of particular resources amongst what may be an object of property. 'Persons' or 'groups of persons' should be taken to include collectivities like the 'public', or a business firm, or the state.

The distribution of responsibilities and liabilities. Included under this heading are both legally enforced responsibilities and legally defined liabilities, and those responsibilities which may not be enforced by law but which may nevertheless be enforced by social convention and public pressure. This item also includes both the responsibilities and liabilities of the person who has the property, and the impositions placed upon others with respect to it. Social expectation may be important. For example, there is a widespread view that persons who own important parts of the 'nation's heritage' should not sell them, export them or deprive others of access to them.

It also needs to be stressed that, as we have seen from an examination of both the jurisprudential treatment of ownership and in the economists' specification of property rights, a crucial liability is to state activity, whether it be taxation, expropriation, or compulsory purchase. Although it is obvious that these sorts of liabilities will vary enormously, a discussion of property which failed to take them into acount would be seriously incomplete. For example, the Conservative government has required local authorities to sell council houses, even if those authorities themselves have no wish to dispose of their housing stock. Councils are in this sense required to sell 'their' property against their will.

Specification of particular interests. A theme in the discussion so far has been the relation between 'ownership' and interests in property which are 'smaller', parts of, or created out of, 'ownership'. If we think the central characteristic of property is that it confers on persons varying degrees of control over or benefit from some resources, these particular interests are legion. An easement, for example, gives a person some interest in another's property. A good example arises when a householder wishes to be connected to a supply line, provided, say, by the gas board. The supply may have to be brought through someone else's land. In such a case, the householder will have to acquire an easement, in this situation a right to bring the gas pipe through. It is worth noting that he acquires no land; and that the gas pipe is not itself his property. The easement is then attached to the householder's property, and may be sold along with the house. The interest the householder acquires is carved out of his neighbour's property, and provides a clear example of the sort of particular interests which can exist.

The extent of the greatest interest. If we follow Honoré in describing 'liberal ownership' as the greatest interest in a thing recognised by a mature legal system, the content of 'greatest interest' will still need to be specified. We have examined Honoré's proposals for such a specification. If we are looking at a system of property either as practised or as recommended, we would want to know about this content. If it varies historically, we shall be faced with a problem in deciding whether we are dealing with a *different* concept of ownership or whether ownership simply did not exist.

One solution to this dilemma is to look for a sufficient set of incidents, and to attribute the position of 'owner' to anyone who holds those particular incidents. Historically, however, this is very unsatisfactory. We may be able to find someone who has rights of use over land, and a right to transfer his use-rights in a will; but the structure of law in which this holding is embedded may not be one which recognised ownership at all, and we shall simply mislead ourselves by employing anachronistic terms. We usually want to know about the social significance of property structures, and we shall not further our enquiries by imposing a definition of ownership upon a set of rights embedded in a social structure which was not attempting to distribute freedom on liberal assumptions.

A parallel point may be made about regarding some set of incidents as sufficient to identify the owner or ownership in a contemporary system. It is an understandable reaction to the messiness produced by fragmentation, by division of the rights and liabilities persons have over resources, to say that we will treat as the owner the person who, although he does not have *all* the incidents enumerated, has a particular set of them. Apart from relying on the misleading idea that 'there is always an owner', and that the problem is to identify him, this approach requires us to select the most significant incidents of ownership. The most significant incidents, however, depend upon the object of property, and often the identity of its holder. It may be, for example, in the case of a productive resource, like land, that we want to know who has the right to its product; but that in the case of a work of art, we want to know who controls access to it. In short, there will always be a certain arbitrariness in designating some particular person 'owner' on the basis of a sub-set of rights and liabilities, which would mislead us historically and distract us from the pattern of particular interests contemporarily. For these reasons, the specification of ownership (in a contemporary system) or of the extent of the greatest interest, is merely part of an enquiry into property, just as 'ownership' is itself a synonym for only one of the meanings of 'property'.

Means available to protect an interest. The existence of a particular interest in a resource is conceptually linked to the means available to protect it. One measure of the extent of an interest is the range of interferences from which protection is provided. This is part of the reasoning behind the attempt to draw a distinction between 'property' and 'contract', and it is related to ideas about absolute ownership understood as an indefeasible title. Such a title would presumably be good against – legally guaranteed against – any rival claim. The means available to a person to protect his interest therefore partly define its extent.

The extent of the protection of an interest may perhaps be conceived in two ways – *de facto* and *de jure*. For example, the protection of copyright in video recordings has recently been enhanced by an Act of Parliament which empowers the police to seize suspected 'pirate' copies. This strengthens the protection of a property right, in a *de jure* sense. By contrast, the police have formed an 'anti-fake squad', to try to prevent the marketing of inauthentic goods represented as being products of particular manufacturers. In as much as this makes existing law more effective in its application, an increase in the *de facto* protection of property interest (in this case trademarks) occurs.

To be comprehensive, consideration of the protection of an interest would also involve consideration of the penalties for interference. For example, someone who smashed up a railway coach in England would usually be prosecuted under laws concerned with criminal damage; but causing damage to state property in the Soviet Union might be treated as sabotage, with correspondingly severe penalties. The size of penalty obviously forms an element in the 'degree' of protection which property enjoys. This protection of an interest is part of the 'social recognition' to which, as we saw above, Pryor draws attention (1973, p.375), and it also helps us to see how lawyers can dispense with the analysis of ownership and property. Very often, all that is required is attention to the means available to protect an interest. A concept of *property* will specify the content of each of these aspects of the notion. If, therefore, we wish to talk about, say, Aristotle's concept of property, we should ideally want to fill in the specified framework. We could then compare concepts of property across different writers, or historical periods. Again, we may examine particular concepts of 'private' and 'public' property by reference to it.

A concept of *ownership* flows from this specification of property but the framework recognises that property and ownership are interchangeable terms only in some contexts. Hence we might discuss the nature of the greatest interest in, say, Roman law. But 'the greatest interest' is only a general phrase; the *content* of the greatest interest may be different between cases we look at, just as the view of justice as 'to each his due' may be filled in by different understandings of the basis on which we work out 'what is due' to a person (needs, rights, desert and so on) (Miller, 1976, pp.20–8).

In the next section we shall examine a debate about the history of
the 'modern' conception of property. This debate has arisen in the
context of a number of books by C. B. Macpherson, which taken
together argue that modern liberal political theory is badly flawed
for reasons which are traceable to possessive assumptions built into
seventeenth-century theories and carried forward to the present
day (Macpherson, 1962, 1973, 1978, 1980; Miller, 1982). According
to Macpherson only three general points can be made about
property. These are, first, that it is a right, not a thing; secondly,
that it is an individual right; and thirdly, that it is an enforceable
claim created by the state (1978, pp.1–13; p.202). Macpherson's
difficulty follows from his attempt to capture the common ground or
general features of property, working from the particular historical
variants which he identifies. In effect, he holds that these three
features are in part common ground between two different
conceptions of property – one embracing common property and one
excluding it; but they are also, in part, products of Macpherson's
preference for one conception of property over another. We can
scarcely fail to notice, however, that even if these three points may
accurately be made of property, they do not distinguish property
from a good deal else. The three points identify property with
individually-held, state-created rights. This characterisation does
not exclude very much, and, incidentally, makes no mention of
duties or liabilities attached to property. We shall later be asking
how Macpherson was led to identify these three features.

This puzzle about the general characterisation is reflected in the
problem of how to identify different conceptions of property, and
how many of them to recognise. Although 'common property' and
'private property' are conceptually distinct, the history of property
is not merely a story of shifts in the degree to which particular
societies recognise one or the other. There are other alterations in
property arrangements to be accommodated. Sometimes these
shifts are considered sufficiently significant as to betoken a new
conception of property. For example, J. G. A. Pocock has
distinguished between the agrarian and mercantile conceptions of
property, suggesting that the latter began to displace the former in
the seventeenth and eighteenth centuries (1976). This is partly a
matter of the prominence of items on a list of property – from land
to negotiable instruments, as it were (Dickson, 1967) – but it also
concerns new ideas about property accompanying that change. In

this example, Pocock's concern is with images of the polity (1979). As these examples show, no-one doubts that the connection between conceptions of property and property institutions is reciprocal and complex.

To acknowledge historical variation in property, then, throws up the problems of identifying the significant variation in institutions and ideas, and relating the two, on the one hand; and of providing a general account of the features of property of which these variants are examples on the other. We have offered such a general account in this section, and in the next we shall look at Macpherson's view of significant change in more detail. We shall then go on to look at a number of other ways in which the history of property has been characterised in order to bring some of the considerations which have been brought to bear on the problem of legitimising property systems.

Debate about the modern concept of property

Clearly one approach to the project of describing how property institutions have changed is to look for the origins of the contemporary view. Three recent contributions have been made to this pursuit, and in principle their conclusions should mesh. In fact however, they are not readily pieced together. The three contributions are Macpherson's attempt to illuminate the history of political thought since the seventeenth century by reference to the notion of possessive individualism; G. E. Aylmer's exploration of the meaning of 'property' in seventeenth-century law dictionaries, which concludes that the idea of absolute ownership became more prominent in that period; and thirdly, the attempt to locate the emergence of the modern concept of ownership in law, and to link it to the findings of legal historians about extensions of owners' powers in the seventeenth century. All three argue for a new conception of property and/or ownership in that period; but the application of the theses differs. Holdsworth (1937) and Milsom (1969), legal historians, were concerned with the content of law. Aylmer (1980) analysed the entries in legal dictionaries. Macpherson concentrated on the assumptions and concepts of political theorists.

The problem of the apparent vacuity of the three general features of property which Macpherson isolates arises from his concern to 'periodise property'. The inelegant phrase is used here to describe various attempts to distinguish historically between varieties of property – as an institution or as an idea. According to Macpherson's (1978) view, two misconceptions about property arose in the seventeenth century. First, property was now treated as a thing not a right. This accompanied the rise of a 'full capitalist market economy' and the 'replacement of old limited rights in land and other valuable things by virtually unlimited rights' (1978, p.7). Secondly, property was newly treated as private property. Before the seventeenth century, property was conceived as either common or private, but in the seventeenth century the idea of common property 'drops virtually out of sight' and was treated 'as a contradiction in terms' (1978, p.10). Because this periodisation embraces property conceived both as private property and as common property, and as both rights and things, Macpherson's treatment of 'property in general' faces a problem. He needs an account of property which covers both periods identified, but he also has preferences between conceptions because he thinks the post-seventeenth century conception imported mistakes. He dismisses the idea that property refers to 'things' rather than to 'rights' partly as a historical misconception (which arose in the seventeenth century and which is being reversed in the twentieth) and partly because it is conceptually inadequate. He thus distinguishes private property, treated as individual rights to exclude others from the benefit and use of something, from common property, treated as individual rights not to be excluded from the benefit and use of something. The addition of the notion that these are enforceable claims created by the state exhausts all that can be said, in Macpherson's view, about property in general. On the basis of this characterisation, Macpherson goes on to prescribe an understanding of property as either an equal right of access to the accumulated means of labour, or as the right to an income from the whole produce of society, underpinning his recommendation with the observation that this is consistent with the three features of property identified (1978, p.206; 1973, p.136).

A major support for the prescription advanced by Macpherson is its alleged compatibility with property as it had been understood between Plato's time and the seventeenth century. This compatibility is desirable because it rejects the narrowing of the meaning of property which occurred in the seventeenth century and which was consonant with a full capitalist market economy. Of course, we can distinguish between the evidence supporting an account of the historically-shifting meanings of property and the use of that evidence to support a prescription, just as we can more generally distinguish between arguments about the history of property and arguments about the legitimacy of property. But clearly, what might be called historical, descriptive accounts are often combined with genetic, normative accounts of the origins of property. Two examples are rival interpretations of the Genesis story of creation, and the debate about the historical status of primitive communism, rejected by Hayek as a socialist myth (1982, vol. 1, p.108).

The clearest account of Macpherson's opinions about the shifting meanings of property occurs in *Democratic Theory*:

> 'When the theory of property is examined, historically and logically, it turns out to be more flexible than the classical liberals or their twentieth-century followers have allowed for. The concept of property has changed more than once, and in more than one way, in the past few centuries. It changed in discernible ways with the rise of modern capitalism, and it is changing again now with the maturation of capitalism.' (1973, p.122)

A 'theory of property', in this context, is 'a theory which both explains and justifies the institution in terms of the purpose served or the need filled' (1973, p.121). Macpherson claims first that the contemporary concept of property emerged in the seventeenth century; secondly, that it is a peculiarly capitalist concept; thirdly that it has begun to change; and finally that it needs to change further (1973, p. 122). Of these disputable claims, we are concerned only with the first two. We have already met one of Macpherson's characterisations of the contemporary concept of property, but in *Democratic Theory* the description is a little more detailed. It is:

> '(a) identical with private property – an individual (or corporate) right to exclude others from the use or benefit of something; (b) a right in or to material things rather than a right to a revenue (and even, in common usage, as the things themselves rather than the rights); and (c) having as its main function to provide an incentive

to labour, as well as (or rather than) being an instrument for the
exercise of human capacities.' (1973, p.122)

The first point to notice is that Macpherson finds it useful to talk
about *the* contemporary concept of property. It is not self-evident
what this is. Would we want to say that there is *a* contemporary
concept of liberty, or several identifiable variants of the notion?
Even those who think that one understanding of liberty is correct or
superior to others recognise the existence of rivals. The same may
well be true of property. Macpherson himself distinguishes
common usage from the ideas of serious thinkers, and perhaps he
could reply that the concept in which he is interested is internal to
liberalism. But it is doubtful whether the concept which is changing
again is one internal to liberalism for it is Macpherson's business to
expose the inadequacies of that liberal concept.

However that may be, the central claims are that this concept is
particularly appropriate to capitalism and that it arose in the
seventeenth century. The theses of the legal historians, and of two
other contributors to the debate, Aylmer and Tuck, may be
compared with these claims. Tuck's (1979) own position is that
while Macpherson is correct in arguing that the 'classic works' had a
'possessive' character – that a person owns his liberty, and other
moral attributes – this was the inevitable consequence of rights
theories which described the possession of a right as dominion over
a moral world (1979, p.3). The major dispute between them is not,
therefore, about the characterisation of seventeenth-century rights
theories as possessive, but about the significance of this feature. For
Tuck, by the mid-fourteenth century, 'The process had begun
whereby all of a man's rights, of whatever kind, were to come to be
seen as his property' (1979, p.16). Tuck's reading of the evidence
has, however, been challenged by Brian Tierney (1983), who
suggests that Tuck has misread the meaning of crucial terms in the
medieval materials. On the other hand, Janet Coleman (1983) has
proposed that John of Paris be regarded as foreshadowing Lockean
possessiveness.

Clearly, there is as yet no agreement about the background to the
possessiveness of the seventeenth-century theories. But there is an
irony here – Macpherson complains about the importation of
possessiveness into liberal political theory yet concludes with a very
broad view of property. It was partly such breadth, according to

Tuck, which was the historical root of the possessiveness of which Macpherson complains.

Apart from this disagreement about datings, what is at stake is partly a matter of how many concepts of property are recognised. Macpherson's procedure is to identify shared and often unspoken assumptions. Tuck's contextual approach exhibits understandings of property by reference to the conflict of ideas. It is not surprising therefore that the one stresses homogeneity while the other stresses multiplicity. Macpherson talks about one concept of property being displaced by another, while Tuck discusses conflict between often co-existing ideas – for example about monastic poverty or freedom of the seas. If we look at the work of the legal historians, which concentrates on a new conception of owners' powers, it appears that some support can be given to the emergence of a novel (but not necessarily dominant) idea of property in seventeenth-century law. It is not clear, however, that this novel conception is particularly appropriate to capitalism.

S. F. C. Milsom has suggested that the powers of owners were increased in that period. The range of persons against whom an owner could assert his proprietorial claims was widened. Milsom thinks that the owner's position was strengthened by an extension of the range of persons he could hold liable to return the value of his property (1969, p.332). Sir William Holdsworth had also detected a change in ideas about ownership in the seventeenth century. On this account, 'the common law had come to recognise that ownership was an absolute right as against all the world, and not merely the better right of a plaintiff as against the defendant in possession' (1937, p.458). This shift was identified with the reception of *dominium* (1937, p.62). Milsom and Holdsworth therefore share the view that ownership was undergoing change, although they do not characterise either the change or its significance in the same ways. G. E. Aylmer's analysis of definitions of property in seventeenth-century law dictionaries suggests two developments. First, the emergence of a definition of absolute individual ownership resting on 'the greatest interest' attributed to the owner, and secondly the erosion of the distinction between real and personal property (1980, pp.96–7). On the face of it, the researches of Milsom, Holdsworth and Aylmer seem to support Macpherson's periodisation. But we should note some qualifications.

First, absolute ownership is not, as we have seen, to be identified with the conception of 'ownership' as the greatest interest. One of the attractions of Honoré's analysis of ownership as 'the greatest interest in a thing recognised by a mature legal system' is that it does not introduce the problem of absolute ownership. It is quite consistent to argue that the owner's powers were increased (the greatest interest, as it were, grew) without supposing that this introduced *dominium*. Milsom accepts the former, but does not, unlike Holdsworth, commit himself to the latter (Reeve, 1980).

Secondly, if we neglect this first qualification and suppose *dominium* was indeed introduced, this will support Macpherson only if the new concept of property he identified has something to do with absolute ownership, (and only if *dominium* is particularly appropriate to capitalism). Macpherson is concerned with the removal of limitations of owners' rights. Milsom suggests an extension of owners' powers but it is not obvious that capitalism is better served thereby. In fact, transfers in specially identified 'open markets' were often exceptions to property rules, because a market collapses if no-one can have confidence in the seller's title. Aylmer noticed the erosion of the distinction between real and personal property. This erosion occurred largely because of the extension of powers of testamentary disposition in land in the sixteenth and seventeenth centuries. This certainly marks an increase in the powers of owners, but it is again not obvious that these are especially consonant with capitalism. One of their consequences was the development of a device to keep land tied up in particular families (Bonfield, 1983), decried in the nineteenth century as a hindrance to the market and, we may therefore suppose, to capitalism.

It is clear, then, that something interesting was happening to ideas about property and ownership with respect to seventeenth-century law. But these are best characterised, with Milsom, as marking an extension of the powers of owners. Confusion arises from running together different kinds of 'extension'. One is an increase in the means to protect an interest – actions available to recover the value of goods. Another is an increase in powers of disposal of property – developments in the testamentary disposition of land. If these are both described as extension of owners' powers, it is tempting to move on to talk of *dominium*. Although capitalism undoubtedly relies upon secure possession and free disposal of property, these developments are not unambiguously supportive of capitalism.

This discussion of aspects of Macpherson's treatment of the history of property illustrates the difficulties identified earlier. First, when does a change in some element of property institutions – in this case the means available to protect an interest and testamentary powers – signal a new conception of property? Secondly, how is the general concept of property offered related to particular variants identified? Here we have seen that Macpherson's general description imports a wide understanding of property similar to that identified by Tuck as a fourteenth-century development, the origin of the possessiveness which Macpherson laments. Thirdly, how is the periodisation identified related to normative enquiries? Clearly for Macpherson the periodisation points to an unwarranted deviation from a broader concept of property, an illegitimate narrowing of its focus which is to be corrected.

In the remainder of the chapter we shall look at other periodisations of property which introduce the themes which are to be explored more fully in subsequent chapters. The other periodisations may be taken in chronological order, because this will enable us to highlight the changing concerns of those who have written about the 'history' of property more easily.

Creation stories and the importance of John Locke

Property institutions are a means by which the control of resources is distributed. To the extent that these resources are primarily or by extension materials of the physical world, thinking about property has been informed by consideration of the origin of the material. This is evidently true of the rival interpretations of the Genesis story, but Creation stories have informed views of property in other religions too. It has been argued that the conflict between European settlers in North America and the Indians already there was rooted partly in different conceptions of property rights and duties, and these different conceptions both turned on religious understandings of the Creation: 'And so, ignoring and desecrating the Indians' reverence for the land, the white settler spread across the plains with his more exploitative ideology. His attitudes were shaped by an anthropocentric religion which demanded that man exercise dominion over the earth and all the lesser creatures' (Large, 1973, p.1043). For the Indian, however, land was incapable of human dominion. 'As long as the sun shines and the waters flow, this land will be here to give life to man and animals. We cannot sell the lives of men and animals; therefore we cannot sell this land. It was put here for us by the Great Spirit and we cannot sell it because it does not belong to us' (p.1042). The first question in exploring the origins of property for a creationist is to sort out the purpose, injunction, or behest of the Creator. If man organises his use of the world partly through a property system, and if both he and the world were created by a god, then the concern with his relationship to the creator will be reflected in the property system regarded as justified.

The basis of what Keith Thomas has described as the 'breathtakingly anthropocentric spirit in which Tudor and Stuart preachers interpreted the biblical story' (1983, p.18) was the same passage from Genesis which occasioned such dispute about the proper relations betwen men ordained by the Creator. 'And God said, Let us make man in our image, after our likeness: and let them have dominion over the fish of the sea, and over the fowl of the air, and over the cattle, and over all the earth, and over every creeping thing that creepeth upon the earth' (1.26). Many questions were asked about this grant: how is man's dominion related to God's? What rights and duties does dominion confer – does it refer to power, or property, or both? To whom exactly is the gift given? Adam's subsequent fate provides a further important element in the theological discussion of property. The subjection of woman to man, the expulsion from the Garden of Eden, necessitating labour, together with the character of fallen man, might all be taken as evidence of the necessity of a particular property system. The possibilities for rival interpretations are increased by the experience of the Flood. When it receded, God blessed 'Noah and his sons' – 'And the fear of you and the dread of you shall be upon every beast of the earth, and upon every fowl of the air, upon all that moveth upon the earth, and upon all the fishes of the sea; into your hand are they delivered' (9.2). Was this a re-affirmation or a fresh beginning? Should its terms be treated as if they were identical with those of the original grant, or an extension of them to encompass now-wild animals with which man previously lived in harmony? And what import does the fact that the grant is to Noah and his sons have for desirable inheritance practices? Were they, from whom 'the whole earth was overspread' (9.19) recipients of a transmissible dominion or propriety, or merely representatives of the human race?

However interpreted, there is usually an implicit and simple periodisation in accounts of the Genesis story. For a version which assumes original communism, in which the world was literally given to all, but which is nevertheless faced by evidence of a contemporary private property system, there are two routes available. One is to seek a legitimating device to show that contemporary private property is justified despite the original communism; that route was followed by, for example, Grotius (1853, vol. 2, p.233) and Pufendorf (1710, p.292), who looked to agreement to provide the legitimation; and by Locke (1965, II, §§26–8), who turned rather to labour. Such procedures required a rather careful statement of the nature of the original communism and the range of powers legitimised by the device. The other route was to see in the disparity between original communism and contemporary private property evidence of the illegitimacy of the latter, and to seek an explanation for the difference. For example, Gerrard Winstanley (1973, p.86) blamed the Norman Conquest for ungodly private property in England in the mid-seventeenth century (Manuel and Manuel, 1979, p.352).

Those who attributed the existence of private property to neither some intervening legitimising device nor to unjustifiable seizure by the powerful might see a connection between the existence of private property and the Fall. They sometimes nevertheless envisaged a period of future communism, when human nature had either been restored or sufficiently restrained to make communism workable. One of the puzzles of More's *Utopia* is to work out which of these possibilities – of restoration or restraint – More placed his hopes on (Kenyon, 1983). He had been deeply influenced by the monastic ideal, in which the absence of private property was supposedly central. Ideas about the appropriate arrangements to govern property in monastic orders had played an important part in the development of Christian thinking about the institution (Tuck, 1979, pp.20–4; Manuel and Manuel, 1979, p.51).

Until the twelfth century, it appears to have been generally agreed that the Genesis story implied original communism and that Apostolic poverty implied the sinfulness of private property, the possession of which was a serious impediment to salvation. According to the accounts given by Sir Richard Southern and Richard Tuck, the development of distinctions between ownership and use, and therefore of ideas about private property, was stimulated by a desire to define just what degree of attachment to private property was defensible for believers in general and monks in particular. Since this may appear a large claim, it is as well to quote directly:

'Down to the twelfth century there was a very meagre theory of property derived from the Bible and the Fathers. The Bible seemed to demand two things: first that men should have a great indifference to property, and secondly, that all property should be held in common. From this it was universally concluded in the early Middle Ages that all private property had the nature of sin, and that in a perfect state there would be no such thing. When St. Benedict included in his Rule the provision that all things were to be held in common, he was expressing not just an ideal for a religious society, but the ideal for all society.' (Southern, 1970, p.53)

Southern points out that Aquinas provided a 'comprehensive defence of private property', but by this time the reception of Aristotle's *Ethics* and *Politics* had suggested a connection between private property and the good life, and the lawyers had developed a distinction between use and ownership. Private ownership might be unobjectionable if there were common use (1970, pp.53–5).

Tuck's exploration of the history of rights theories gives a much more detailed account of the importance of this distinction between use and ownership. And Tuck (1979) points out that Aquinas was able to talk of a natural dominion over objects through the use man could put them to: and this is part of his novel 'comprehensive defence' of private property. The concept of *dominium utile* which enabled Aquinas to mount this defence was also the ground for treating all rights as property rights, a development we have already mentioned in connection with the dispute about its dating. In Tuck's view, 'the recognition of the category of *dominium utile* was to transform rights theories. For now *dominium* was taken to be any *ius in re*: *any* right which could be defended against all other men, and which could be transferred or alienated by its possessor, was a *property* right, and not only rights of total control' (1979, p.16).

One interpretation of Genesis was capable of avoiding a contrast between how matters were in the beginning, or what they might become, and the contemporary existence of private property. That argument was put by Sir Robert Filmer (1949), and simply denied that there had ever been a time when private property was absent. The grant of dominion to Adam was of property and authority, subsequently transmitted through the generations. In articulating his objections to Filmer's account, Locke went beyond the dichotomy of common property and private property, to suggest a mechanism for the development of the latter, which was extended by Smith and others in the next century.

Filmer was rejecting the arguments of Grotius and Pufendorf. Grotius thought his account of the origins of private property, by agreement, to be in accord with 'the sacred history, sufficiently agreeing with the account given by philosophers and poets' (1853, vol. 2, p.238) – the polite term for pagans. The fundamental assertion was that: 'God gave the human race generally a right to the things of a lower nature, at the Creation, and again, after the Deluge. Every thing was common and undivided, as if all had one patrimony' (1853, vol. 2, p.228). Filmer favoured Selden's view, that God's grant had been to Adam, but he dissociated himself from Selden's idea that the grant to Noah was to be held in common with the sons (1949, pp.63–4). His arguments against the Grotian account were first, the lack of evidence for consent as the basis of private property and secondly, the problem of reconciling the notion that all were born free and equal with the obligations imposed on subsequent generations by the consent of their forebears. 'These and many more absurdities', he wrote, 'are easily removed if we maintain the natural and private dominion of Adam to be the foundation of all government and propriety' (1979, p.71).

Locke's procedure for avoiding the absurdities pointed out by Filmer involved a labour theory of property entitlement and a different specification of inheritance as a natural right. Appropriation from the common stock without consent yet constrained by the law of nature was envisaged as occurring in stages, exercised initially over the fruits of the earth and later over the land itself. The constraints required an appropriator to avoid anything 'wasting' in his possession, and to leave 'enough and as good' for others (1965, II, §§31–7). The later use of money both introduced inequalities in holdings and had harmful effects on man's character (II, §§46–50). Locke was certainly not the first to think in terms of stages of appropriation: the separation between fruits of the earth, the land and money was common. But Locke may reasonably be seen as providing a pivot between the exegetical and justificatory theological distinction (of common or undifferentiated patrimony from private property) on one side, and theories of social development (like Adam Smith's) on the other, for Locke conceived of the development of property as a natural process. The tone of this passage from Vaughn (1980, p.81) captures the point, although perhaps not everything said in it is defensible. 'In Locke's state of nature, people work, gather food, sow and reap, hire servants, create and use tools, exchange the products of their labor with one another and, eventually, use money. Not only do all these activities take place, but they lead to economic growth and the development of economic institutions which finally become incompatible with the continuation of a state of nature.' The idea that it is economic growth and development which leads to the introduction of civil society, presumably to protect the growing holdings of property from the 'quarrelsome and contentious' (II, §34) avoids one problem in Lockean commentary. That is to reconcile statements that the state of nature is fairly harmonious with less sanguine remarks about the need for government. It is the marriage between this story of economic development and the theologically-informed discussion of property which entitles Locke to some sort of pivotal position in the practice of periodising property.

Locke famously remarked that a mere day labourer in England is better fed and clad than the king of an American tribe (II, §42). He appeared to deny the importance of inequality by pointing to the minimum level of welfare achieved. The contrast between England and America, for Locke, turns on the lack of incentive to lay out labour where there is no money. It might not be too fanciful to regard the welfare level as the unintended consequence of the use of money. Money encourages the more intensive use of resources like land, but there is no suggestion that anyone had in mind the overall result of the process when giving tacit consent to its use. Its use does, though, help individuals to accumulate without violating the natural law provisions governing appropriation. One piece of evidence for Locke's dual or pivotal position – between the theological concern and the developmental one – concerns this view of 'American' subsistence. The theological account usually treated early society as exhibiting a variety of property forms, in deference to the occupations of Cain and Abel. Locke mentions that account, but also the alternative view that 'in the beginning all the world was America' (II, §49) where the Indian is a tenant in common (Meek, 1976, pp.21–2).

Adam Smith and social development

Adam Smith (1976, pp.23–4) used a similar comparison between a frugal peasant and the king of an African tribe, attributing the different levels of welfare achieved to the development of the division of labour in the one case and its absence in the other. But he also extended the discussion of the origins of property in his remarks on the four stages of social organisation. The four stages are those of hunting, flock-tending, agriculture and commerce. Property and its development are involved in a complicated way in both the characterisation of the stages and the assessment of their benefits or draw-backs (Skinner, 1982).

Smith's (1978, p.8) definition of property was narrower than that of most seventeenth-century authors. Locke (1965, II §87n) amongst others had used property to mean 'life, liberty and estate', and Hobbes (n.d., p.224) had thought that conjugal affection was one of the forms of property most dear to a man. Smith, however, classified the injuries to which men are liable as arising from interference with body, reputation or estate. Property was accounted merely as part of this last category. Rights to body and reputation were natural, but those to estate were acquired (1978, p.105). This apparently clear position is muddled somewhat in various ways: in particular, Smith (1978, p.105) sometimes wrote as if all acquired rights were property, and, as we shall see later, he seemed to recognise some sort of natural claim to property in labour. One natural origin for possession which he did recognise was the hunter's right to his prey (1978, p.207); but this was not a natural right to property, because the hunter was treated as having only an exclusive privilege (1978, p.107). Indeed, in the hunting stage, according to Smith, the idea of property was absent, and possession was all.

One aspect of his enterprise was to explain how property developed:

> 'The origin of natural rights is quite evident. That a person has a right to have his body free from injury, and his liberty free from infringement unless there be a proper cause, no body doubts. But acquired rights such as property require more explanation. Property and civil government very much depend on one another. The preservation of property and the inequality of possession first formed it, and the state of property must always vary with the form of government.' (1978, p.401)

Three aspects of the involvement of property in the stadial thesis are of interest here. First, what is an object of property to some extent characterises the stages; secondly, modes of acquisition vary between and within stages; and thirdly, although the power and authority of government and the level, distribution and security of property influence each other, the manner in which that influence operates changes.

First, then, types of property increase in the sense that the list of objects of property is extended. In the hunting stage there is, as we have seen, no property; matters are regulated by some natural idea of possession and exclusive privilege. Smith locates two extensions of property which he regards as highly significant, although their relative importance is perhaps unclear. The emergence of the shepherd stage is said (1978, p.20) to be an *extension* of property, although he sometimes more consistently regards it as the *introduction* of property: 'Settled laws therefore, or agreements concerning property, will soon be made after the commencement of the age of shepherds' (1978, p.209). This extension is reinforced by shepherds treating possession not only as a matter of what they have about them, but also what they have in their hovels (1978, p.460). Hence the move from a hunting society to a shepherd society is said to be of major import: 'The step betwixt these two is of all others the greatest in the progression of society, for by it the notion of property is extended beyond possession, to which it is in the former state confined' (1978, p.107). 'The greatest extension of property' is elsewhere (1978, p.460) attributed to the introduction of agriculture, so the relative significance of the two extensions is hazy. But the central point is plain; in the first three stages, property is first treated as only possession, then animals become objects of property, and later land itself does. This differentiation between the stages leads naturally to the question of whether there is another extension of property with the introduction of the commercial stage. What marks the fourth stage, however, is not extension conceived as a new object of property but extension in the sense of diffusion.

The mode of acquisition of property and the range of powers a property owner has vary between and within stages. This is partly a consequence of the extension of property to animals and land, but it is also related to the principles of authority which are associated with each stage.

Smith (1978, p.63) finds something puzzling in inheritance practices, since they are unnecessary to the constitution of property but (once again) an extension of it, as these three quotations make plain: 'All laws which extend property beyond the person of the possessor are of later introduction than those which constitute property, and are not at all necessary to its existence' (1978, p.309). 'It is to be observed that there is no extension of property so great as this, and therefore it was long before it could be introduced; it was very natural to give a man a right to dispose of his property while he lived, but a testament supposes him to dispose of a right when properly speaking he can have none himself' (1978, p.466). 'The greatest of all extensions of property is that by entails. To give a man power over his property after his death is very considerable, but it is nothing to an extension of this power to the end of the world' (1978, p.467). The reader is by now beginning to lose count of greatest extensions. Nevertheless the development of inheritance institutions is clear enough: property becomes transmissible, in the shepherd stage, but the association of property with particular families for great periods – the purpose of entail – is concentrated in the feudal period, a phase of the agricultural stage. One characteristic of commercial society is the absence of that association, and Smith regards entail in such a society as an obstructive hangover from an earlier period (1976, pp.382–5; 1978, pp.68–70).

This connection between entail and feudalism brings us to the third concern, the relationship between government and the security, level and distribution of property. The relationship is reciprocal: 'the form of government' affects the 'state of property' and *vice versa*. In the hunting stage there is no property and very little government; but government is made necessary by disputes occasioned by property in the shepherd stage, where wealth is the basis of political authority and where inequality in property has its greatest impact in creating power based on the dependence of the poor. The agricultural stage initially contains allodial property, later feudal – a change which Smith locates between the ninth and eleventh centuries (1978, p.52, pp.244–5). The development of the commercial stage from the late feudal is tied up with the growth of arts, commerce and luxury. Smith looks at the interaction of the king, nobles and others, resulting in greater independence for vassals and burghers (1978, pp.259–61). The expenditure of the nobles' surplus revenues on the products of art – usually in towns where merchants might also import luxuries – led to a dissipation of power accruing from large numbers of retainers (1978, p.26). The central proposition is that large property holdings produce a greater share of power in societies where 'arts are uncultivated' (1978, pp.49–50) than in those where they are. Commercial society, where arts are widely pursued, therefore reduces inequality in power. 'This manner of laying out ones money is the chief cause that the balance of property confers so small a superiority of power in modern times' (1978, p.50). Compared to the shepherd stage, in which wealth gave immediate power, or to the feudal period, in which property in land produced armies of retainers and family birth was important, commercial society diffuses property and defuses its connection with power.

The transition from feudal to commercial society is caused largely by the trading activities of town dwellers. The activities of merchants who bring in luxuries and of artisans who produce goods are reasons for the decline of the feudal system. This picture of the actual history of commercial society is, for Smith, to be contrasted with the 'natural progress' of economic activity, which would have been initially agricultural, supplemented by manufacturing and finally developed by commerce. In fact, commerce had stimulated agriculture, which had originally been disrupted by the distribution of all land, cultivated or not, following conquest, and the insulation of land from the market by inheritance institutions. Greater security and fixed money rents gave farmers an incentive to improve cultivation. Although there is a clear but varying connection between property and power in the four stages, there is also a causal link between military power and the structure of property institutions. As Smith noted then, 'property and civil government very much depend on one another.'

Property, then, plays an important part in Smith's conjectural history. First, the hunting stage is marked by an absence of property; the shepherd stage by its introduction; the agricultural by fixed property in land. Secondly, the powers of property holders change as both sentiment and material possibility suggest their appropriateness – hence wills, originally unknown in the shepherd stage, are introduced, and primogeniture and entail are used to keep blocks of resources intact. Lastly, although the preservation of property is the motive for the introduction of government, the commercial stage is marked by the wide distribution of property and the attenuation of the hitherto direct connection between property and power. Smith's general stadial theory has attracted attention partly as presaging Marx's account of modes of production (Skinner, 1982). Scholars have argued about its originality and its ubiquity, and looked for its antecedents. Our concern with 'property' is narrower; and the comparison between Locke and Smith is illuminating in this context.

Both Locke and Smith present a 'natural' history of property institutions, but, of course, they are asking different questions about that history. Locke is asking, how could private property have arisen legitimately? Smith is asking, how has commercial society arisen, and how are differences between it and previous social forms to be explained? In Locke's theory behaviour is to be regulated by a law of nature guiding the rational and industrious; in Smith's, self-interest generates development in social institutions. Locke starts from natural property rights, the existence of which Smith apparently rejects.

Nevertheless there are parallels within these differences. Although Smith does not discuss the origins of legitimate property, the sense in which it has natural origins is so strong that legitimacy is thereby suggested. Smith's critical remarks on institutions and policy also make it plain that he has definite ideas on what is legitimate. For example, of the ways by which property may be acquired that he identifies, occupation and accession are regarded as original, while the others are secondary (1978, p.27). They are original in two senses. Something like occupation regulates possession among hunters, and accession is presumably vital to animal breeding amongst shepherds' stocks. But the second sense is of what would be natural and generally accord with sentiment – which is why testamentary disposition is regarded as a late development, since there is nothing obvious about it. Again, 'The property which every man has in his own labour, as it is the original foundation of all other property, so it is the most sacred and inviolable' (1976, p.138). Hindering a man from employing his labour by improper regulations is therefore unjust. Similarly Smith (1976, p.572) approves the colony law which takes away property in land which has been uncultivated, a provision Locke included in the *Fundamental Constitutions of Carolina*. Indeed, Smith is against the practice of entail because it violates the accepted maxim 'that the earth is the property of each generation' (1978, p.69).

A second parallel within the apparent differences is that it is clear that both Locke and Smith have in mind a sort of natural process, in which developing appropriation has assignable causes and effects. Skinner usefully distinguished the comparative statics of Smith's discussion from its dynamics (1982, pp.87–90). One aspect of the dynamic, common to both theories, is constant human nature operating in changing circumstances to produce a result which particular individuals neither foresaw nor intended. In Locke's theory, the satisfaction of need leads to appropriation of the fruits of the earth and the land; money is recognised as useful and population growth stimulates trade to produce unequal holdings of private property. For Smith, too, appropriation would naturally develop on a particular path, although in fact that natural course had been altered. The dynamics of this natural course are not very clear, but they seem to rely on the increased difficulty of gaining subsistence.

The comparative statics of the analysis of the four stages underpin Smith's conception of desirable property arrangements. The system of natural liberty which helps a commercial society to flourish is also made possible by commercial society. Hence a well-constructed commercial policy enables men to use their property in their labour, is suspicious of patents, copyrights and monopolies and detests inheritance institutions which keep landed property in a few hands (1978, p.83, p.363; 1976, pp.384–5). The desirability of particular property systems, then, is implicitly informed by an understanding of the consequences of alternative variants in other stages, particularly for the distribution of power. Locke, by contrast, explicitly uses the comparative static comparison to underpin his discussion of legitimate property.

Locke, then, was writing a history of property to show how it could have arisen legitimately. Smith was writing a conjectural history of society in which the development of property was assumed to have a natural course. In the nineteenth century, under the impact of Darwinian perspectives, this natural course was itself treated as an evolution (Bock, 1979). In this connection we have already encountered *The Evolution of Property from Savagery to Civilisation*. But perhaps the most extraordinary example of this genre is Charles Letourneau's account *Property, its Origin and Development* published in 1892. Although Letourneau certainly does not have the importance of Locke, Smith or Marx, it is worth glancing at his ideas partly to see how approaches to the history of property have changed and partly to facilitate the comparison between his evolutionary approach and that based upon modes of production.

Evolution and modes of production

Letourneau protested that the ethnography which existed shortly before he wrote was defective because of its limited sources, and that the theory of stages built upon it was incorrect. 'Not very long ago, when ethnography confined itself to the Bible and classical antiquity, it was confidently assumed that man, always and everywhere, had begun by being a hunter, was next a shepherd, then an agriculturalist. Now we can no longer accept this gradation' (1892, p.90). His main objection to the hunter–shepherd–agriculturalist story was the economists' mistaken idea that private property arose from work. Although he was prepared to concede that the 'psychic origin of private property' was a consequence of 'personal work, of the manufacture of weapons and utensils, fashioned by their owner, and buried or burnt with him; but this idea' was in fact 'extended to all articles, to all beings, that the individual appropriated or retained for his own benefit, whatever the origin of their appropriation' (1892, p.91). The place given to animals in Smith's theory, the first possession capable of large scale accumulation and transmission as the foundation of power, is taken by slaves in Letourneau's account. Private property had its origin not in work but in 'violence and usurpation' since the captive who was not killed, *qua* slave, constituted the first important capital (1892, p.90).

Since Letourneau felt able to identify property among animals and since he wanted to trace the development of property from the beginning until his own day, his book is replete with wearisome detail which we may pass over. His general thesis is this. The origin of property is to be found in an instinct for preservation, socialised among the first men who grouped themselves in hordes and lived by hunting. Everything was held in common, especially the land itself. Weapons and ornaments which a person made were thought of as part of him; and this connection between maker and object was confounded with that between appropriator and object appropriated. Hence women and slaves taken in conquest marked the establishment of a right of private property. The development of agriculture, including both pasturage and cultivation, made it necessary to define a right of property in land: first common cultivation, then family usufruct with periodic re-allotment. This family usufruct became transmissible family property; village communities resulted and within villages more and more land was taken as private property transmissible within the family. Although this process was interrupted in societies which developed feudalism, the motor of it, namely 'individualism' eventually undermined feudalism too. The result of all this was profound inequality of fortune in the Europe of his own day: this was a stage, Letourneau thought, which had been reached by other civilisations, and was associated with their destruction by conquest. In contemporary Europe, however, he hints darkly, the barbarians may well be within.

Here Letourneau's thesis turns out to have a moral. His story of the destruction of communal sentiment, originally embodied in communal property but finally engulfed by inequality of private fortune, especially in land, is partly didactic. Social facts, he holds, are modifiable, and the urgent necessity is to reduce inequality through a steeply graduated tax on inheritance. The lessons of the past must be learned before it is too late (1892, pp.364–98).

Although Letourneau was slightly mocking about the ethnography of those who took the Bible and ancient societies as their sources, the general pattern of his view of the development of property does not diverge very sharply from Smith's. His objection to the hunting–pastoral–agricultural–modern model was merely that the pastoral phase was not universal, that keeping animals and tilling land went hand in hand. So where Smith had attributed great importance to property in animals, Letourneau, denying the distinctive character of a pastoral phase, thought the first emergence of property as capital occurred with slave-agriculture. The characterisation of the process of development of property, however, was unequivocal. It was a general and relentless movement away from common property which had run its course with disastrous results for particular civilisations in the past and which threatened contemporary Europe. The diffusion of property and power which Smith thought possible in commercial society was absent in an industrial one and rampant individualism led to great inequality and the unjust suffering of the propertyless.

Obviously, modern social science would have grave doubts about both Letourneau's methods and the quality of his data, and would be extremely sceptical about whether there is a history of property in this general sense at all. The existence of such a history, for Letourneau, discloses a cycle of progressive as well as possessive individualism, evident in the history of property institutions of particular civilisations, such that co-existing societies may be taken as evidence of stages through which the most advanced have passed, confirmed against the actual history of the most advanced societies wherever possible. This comparative procedure was also adopted by Lafargue (1975, p.9). Letourneau's history claims that the development of the unrestrained and selfish right of private property can everywhere be traced and that it has been the main cause of the ruin of civilisations.

The evolutionary ethnography of Letourneau may be compared with Paul Lafargue's account in *The Evolution of Property*. Lafargue restricted his study to the movement from 'savagery to civilisation', while Letourneau talked about property among animals. But the shared evolutionary perspective hides one significant difference, namely that Lafargue wrote with a commitment to a particular understanding of history. In fact, he used a quotation from *Capital* as a scene-setter for his essay: 'The economic structure of society is the real basis on which the juridical and political superstructure is raised, and to which definite social forms of thought correspond: in short the mode of production determines the character of the social, political and intellectual life generally' (facing p.1). Lafargue wanted to write the history of property before it had adopted its contemporary form, capital. His adoption of the quotation as a banner indicates clearly enough a desire to place that history within the general historical interpretation offered by Marx. Unfortunately, commentators have been puzzled by the place of 'property' in Marx's treatment of modes of production and of history. But some have connected Marx's account fairly closely to Adam Smith's historical typology, and we must now explore two related issues: first, how does Marx conceive of property within his theory of history? Secondly, to what extent does his conception differ from that of Adam Smith?

R. L. Meek has argued for the profound importance of Smith's account of 'stages' in the following way:

> 'The theory was that society "naturally" or "normally" progressed over time through more or less distinct and consecutive stages, each corresponding to a different mode of subsistence, these stages being defined as hunting, pasturage, agriculture and commerce. To each of these modes of subsistence . . . there correspond different sets of ideas and institutions relating to law, property, and government and also different sets of customs, manners and morals. [The] four stages theory . . . was destined not only to dominate socio-economic thought in Europe in the latter half of the eighteenth century, but also to become of crucial significance in the subsequent development of economics, sociology, anthropology, and historiography, right down to our own time.' (1976, p.2)

This interpretation talks of the correspondence between ideas relating to property and the mode of subsistence. This, of course, requires a specification of modes of subsistence which is independent of ideas relating to property. But, as we have seen, the first three stages seem to be important to Smith because of the forms which property adopts in them. In other words, we might interpret Smith in a rather different way to Meek, holding that Smith is designating different types of property with which a mode of subsistence is associated, and to which different structures of power and authority correspond. The fourth stage, commercial society, is defined by reference to the ubiquity of markets and the diffusion of property. Meek's account makes property secondary to a mode of subsistence, but Smith's ideas about a 'mode of subsistence' seem to depend on the form of property. To put the point differently, Meek's characterisation of Smith's hypothetical history, suggesting a correspondence between modes of subsistence and ideas about property, seems to read Marx back into Smith. As Bradley and Howard point out, however, '. . . Marx tied in this conception [the materialist conception of history] with the analysis of the surplus much more explicitly and systematically than did Smith. Marx developed typologies of economic structures in which the method of extraction was *the* defining quality' (1982, p.6). We must now look at the place of property in these typologies.

In *The German Ideology*, the historical account provided by Marx and Engels does follow Smith's fairly closely. Tribal (hunting and fishing), shepherd and agricultural arrangements are discussed. Simon Clarke has commented that *The German Ideology* (1846) 'hardly goes beyond' the account given by Smith and developed by Ferguson and Millar (1982, p.44). Bradley and Howard use typologies worked out from the basis of the extraction of surplus to distinguish Marx from Smith, and they presumably have in mind *The Communist Manifesto* (1848) and the *Preface to a Critique of Political Economy* (1859). In the *Manifesto* ancient, feudal and capitalist modes are discussed. In the *Preface* Asiatic, ancient, feudal and modern bourgeois modes of production are designated. And, of course, socialism as a future 'mode of production' or, at least, form of society must be included. Marx also recognised a form of primitive communism in prehistorical society. It is in these latter accounts of the historical theory that commentators have found particular difficulty with the place of property.

Marx and Engels described all hitherto existing societies as class societies and classes were defined by reference to the means of production (1977, p.222). The future classless society is one in which private ownership of the means of production has been abolished. The Asiatic mode, in which there is no such private ownership, therefore has an ambiguous status. As Moore points out, the recognition of such a society is incompatible with the definition of class society taken with the assertion that *all* hitherto existing societies were class societies (1980, pp.214–15). Looked at in terms of ownership of the means of production, the ancient, feudal and capitalist modes, on one side, are characterised by 'private' ownership of those means, while the Asiatic and future models are characterised by its absence. Taken with 'primitive communism', the general movement is from common property through private property and back to common property. But more is needed to distinguish particular modes of production.

One way of providing further distinctions within the modes of production in which there is private property is to look at the means by which surplus is extracted from the producers. The direct character of that extraction is clear in slave societies and in feudal society, but in capitalism the extraction is less obvious. Marx's project was to reveal the process by which the apparently equal exchange of labour power for wages nevertheless made possible the self-expansion of capital through the appropriation of surplus value. The classification by reference to the method of extraction is no doubt what Bradley and Howard had in mind when they drove a wedge between Smith and Marx. Marx's 'typologies of economic structures', we recall, make 'the method of economic extraction *the* defining quality'. Slavery, feudalism and capitalism represent different methods of extraction. Unlike the typology in *The German Ideology*, this does not rest on forms of property like land and animals. But property is obviously involved in the characterisation of the modes of production despite that. Slavery involves property in persons, and capitalism contains a proletariat which has no property other than its labour power. Feudalism has no proletariat, a group which exists entirely by the sale of its labour power. A good deal of the analysis of the origins of capitalism has to do with the process by which the future proletariat was separated from the means of production in which it had hitherto had some property. But feudalism does not depend upon slavery either: for that requires a group which *is* property and therefore owns no property, subject, even for life itself, to other persons.

The superiority of future Communist society, for Marx, would be partly its propertylessness, in the sense of the absence of individual ownership, at least in the means of production: 'From the standpoint of a higher economic form of society, private ownership of the globe by single individuals will appear as absurd as private ownership of one man by another' (1974, vol. 3, p.776). Marx's theory of history, then, is concerned with modes of production. One theme is the emergence of private property from primitive communism, and the hope that private property will, in the future, be overthrown by the proletarian revolution, which will put an end to all forms of class society. Although class society is associated with the absence of both communal ownership and communal control of the means of production, the forms of that sort of society are further distinguished by the method of extraction adopted. The questions which have provoked controversy about this analysis are legion, but two are particularly important with respect to property and arise from within the theory of history. A problem within the general theory is whether it makes sense to divide social life into parts, and to talk of one part determining, corresponding to, or conditioning the other. The two particular questions for a theory of property are to decide, first, where 'property' would fit into such a division and secondly where it would fit into any dynamic which carried societies from one mode of production to another.

The phrases 'determine', 'condition' and 'correspond to' are all taken from a short passage in the so-called *1859 Preface*. This 'summary statement' of the materialist conception of history has raised many problems: is it an hypothesis, or a fully-fledged theory? Which term (determine, condition, correspond to) would Marx want to commit himself to? (Cohen, 1978; Carver, 1982). Whilst a review of these issues would take us away from our present concerns, we may attend to the clear and careful exposition of one of the problems given by Michael Evans, which is directly relevant to arguments about the history of property. It also draws attention to a theme in this essay, that the complexity of discussion of 'property' arises from its dual character as a description of physical relations to resources and jural relations.

Evans sets the problem out in this way:

'Marx states that the labour process is always carried on within and through a specific social form, by which he chiefly means a property system. Participation in production involves production relations, which involve both work relations and ownership relations. But Marx goes further, and claims that production determines the property system which is part of production. If production is used in a wide sense (involving the technical work process *plus* property relations), then the claim is of the form $P(A+B)$ determines B, which is unenlightening, not to say tautological. If production is used in a narrow sense (involving the technical work process only), then the claim is of the form $P(A)$ determines B, which is not tautological and entails a technological determinism. The latter claim makes sense and is false.' (1975, pp.68–9)

In other words, if the 'mode of production' means work relations and property relations, the claim that the mode of production determines property relations is uninteresting. If, however, the mode of production means only work relations, then the claim that the mode of production determines property relations is interesting but, on reflection, untrue, since we know of societies which employ similar work relations and have quite different property systems. Without pursuing all the ramifications of this, we should note that it is not clear how Marx's historical periodisation locates property relations: whether they are part of the system of production, or in some way a consequence of it.

This problem is made more acute by consideration of the dynamic of Marx's historical schema. A transition from one social form to another is effected, he held, by the forces of production breaking through the relations of production. At least, this is how he put the matter when he discussed the supersession of capitalism. The forces of production would, he thought, develop to a point at which the relations of production, and in particular private ownership of the means of production, would not be sustainable. As Moore has pointed out, the account in the *Preface* seems to equate relations of production with property relations (1980, p.222). Since this contrast is run together with that between economic base and superstructure, commentators have been puzzled as to whether the property relations are part of the base or of the superstructure. Moore's criticism of Marx's lack of clarity refers to the dynamic of movement between modes of production; Evans's discussion is concerned with the delineation of a social form. The two are related by uncertainty about the status of property. According to Moore:

'The crucial difference between bourgeois and proletarian revolutions, as these are described in the *Manifesto*, concerns the role of property relations. In the transition from feudalism to capitalism, property relations constitute part of the base: bourgeois revolution consists primarily in adjusting political institutions to a changed economic system [. . .] But in the transition from capitalism to socialism, property relations do not constitute part of the base: proletarian revolution consists

primarily in adjusting both political and economic institutions to
a changed technology.' (1980, p.224)

Moore argues, then, that Marx could not consistently place
property in the superstructure because his account of the
emergence of capitalism from feudalism relies on the development
of capitalist property relations *before* the bourgeois revolution. In
the case of the transition to socialism, property relations are altered
by the abolition of private property in the means of production *after*
the revolution. While slavery and capitalism can be partly
characterised by property relations – property in the slave, and the
proletariat's lack of property in the means of production – the
problem is to find an equivalent for feudalism. The obvious
candidate would be customary claims on the labour of others –
either to their time or produce. This system of manorial obligations
fell into disuse before the bourgeois revolution. This point
strengthens Moore's case that the transition from feudalism to
capitalism is effected by changes in the relations of production (for
him, property relations) before the superstructural change.

We may thus conclude our discussion of Marx's historical
typology. It was enunciated in his earlier formulation, *The German
Ideology*, in terms close to those employed by Adam Smith. We
saw, however, that Smith did not make any sharp claims about the
relationship between property and the mode of subsistence on one
side, and the arrangement of power and authority on the other. He
seems to have thought that there would be developments in the
form which property adopted, and consequent changes in the
principles of authority. Nevertheless, the form of property played
only a part in distinguishing the modes of subsistence, and 'the
consequent change' was to do with sentiments of appropriateness as
well as material possibility. When Marx moved beyond a similar
typology, he distinguished within the period of class society and
'private' property in the means of production by reference to the
methods employed to extract surplus. But in the characterisation of
modes of production he left the place of property unclear (so that
we are unsure whether it is part of that which determines or
conditions something else) and in his discussion of the dynamics of
movement between feudalism and capitalism, and capitalism and
socialism, he seems to first exclude property relations from the
superstructure and then to include them within it.

The overall pattern of Marx's periodisation is clear enough: from primitive communism, through various forms of class society, to a future classless society where communism has again been established. The general pattern reproduces the hope that fallen man, labouring under a system of private property, will one day be sufficiently reformed or restored to enjoy God's grant in common. To say this is not to equate Marx's notion of future society with either millenarianism or utopianism. It simply draws attention to structural similarity in periodisations of property, and to the complex interplay of historical description and normative commitment which they embody.

Property, in the interpretations of Genesis, was first and foremost distinguished by the content of God's gift. Resources of use to man could be organised in common or exclusively, and the intention of the gift, in all versions, helped to define the rights and duties of individuals. Since, however, man was part of the created world, a question about his status with respect to these resources arose naturally. As an organiser of material, man reproduced the activities of a creative God; but his position as part of the creation rested on a special gift to him, and the terms of this gift defined the nature of legitimate property relations. Rival interpretations produced different ideas of legitimate property, but no-one disputed the normative consequences of the particular historical interpretation offered, and everyone agreed that the important question was whether the original gift had been in common, and if so whether private property could be legitimate.

Locke's approach to this problem is of special interest because he moved beyond the distinction between common and private property as forms of the gift and worked out a story of the development or extension of private property as well. Locke was not, of course, unique merely because of this, since Grotius and Pufendorf also saw the emergence of private property as incremental. Things immediately of use for life were first divided, to be followed later by other resources, as inclination and dispute suggested. Indeed, both Grotius (1853, vol. 2, p.232) and Pufendorf (1710, p.293f) recognised a sort of economic motive for division; for Grotius, the choice of a more refined mode of living, and for Pufendorf a similar inclination coupled with a desire to benefit from one's own exertions. But although these writers might identify an economic *motive*, they treated the legitimacy of division as a matter of agreement. Locke, famously, did not: his legitimising device, the expenditure of labour, required no agreement, and as a result he was able to characterise the development of property as a *natural economic process*. In this respect, the connections between the juristic claims of labour and the value added or created by labour are still not adequately explained. Locke's story of the origins of private property is of a process in which self-interested men interact to produce a result which no-one intends, a result which is used to legitimise the process itself.

Smith's account extends the emphasis on social development. For Meek, the special feature of the stadial thesis in Smith's hands is that it is no longer a story about changes in property alone, but rather about changes in social organisation generally, especially since 'property and government very much depend on one another.' Apart from the process which underlies the differentiation of property, Locke and Smith share the view that the development of property can be exhibited as an extension of ideas about the connection between the person and the object. The proper limits of this association between person and object are exceeded, Smith held, by inheritance institutions which allow a man to reach too far into the future. Letourneau sees the history of property as a consequence or form of growing individualism. Locke's developmental story unites forms of private property as extensions of the act of labour. For Smith, important changes in property involve extensions of the sentiment of association. In all these cases, private property is 'naturalised' as an extension or development of an original act of appropriation.

We may distinguish between two accounts of the history of property in Marx's writings – that in the *German Ideology* which is at least similar to Adam Smith's in outline, and that developed later. In the later versions, Marx's account may be related to problems identified earlier in the following way. First, how are changes in ideas and institutions related, and the significant ones chosen? The theory of modes of production looks helpful but we have seen that the place of property or property relations in that theory is difficult to establish both for any particular mode of production and for the dynamic replacement. Secondly, how is property-in-general treated? Marx would probably not have found this a very interesting question, preferring to discuss it in a concrete social setting. But his history of methods of production does have normative implications for property arrangements. Since common property is an original condition and since the absence of common property is associated with various forms of class society, common property is recommended as appropriate to the classless society with the proletarian revolution is held to inaugurate.

Conclusion

We may address the question of the contemporary political significance of these approaches to the history of property in a number of ways. Three examples may be mentioned. First, a political theory such as Marxism, when harnessed to action, has given rise to particular forms of property system (although not necessarily the *same* property system) in many countries of the contemporary world. Secondly, many of the ideas contained in these theories form part of the collective inheritance of political theory (even if we reject Macpherson's account of the ideas and of the consequent poverty of modern liberal theory). Thirdly, ideas based on an interpretation of Genesis, or more generally of God's purposes for man, have not only informed both conservative and radical political thought, but also are reflected in modern ideas about property institutions appropriate to imperfect human nature. We shall return to these points in later chapters.

In general, the relationship between the history of property and arguments about its legitimacy is as follows. First, the supposed actual history of property does not entail any particular view about desirable property arrangements, inasmuch as there is a logical gap between what *is* and what *should be* the social practice. Secondly, however, a view of what *has been* is likely to figure in a story of what *should be*; the dispute about primitive communism, for example, is partly a dispute about the *possibility* of a society without private property. Although the legitimacy of property can be discussed without reference to historical concerns, the question of how legitimate property could possibly arise cannot be ignored; and then the connection between actual history and hypothetical history may become unclear. While in principle the history of property could be non-normative, and arguments about the legitimacy of property could be non-historical, the question of how property could legitimately arise brings the historical and normative concerns together again.

In this chapter we have met a number of considerations which have been brought to bear on the discussion of desirable property institutions, and some may appear less relevant to our contemporary circumstances than others. For example, the notion that what is required is to be discovered by biblical interpretation may not seem as compelling today as it did in the seventeenth century (which is not to deny that for many people, consistency with the requirements of God is still a major determinant of the value of social institutions). But we can, a-historically, detach many considerations from the framework in which they were embedded. For example, Locke aimed to design a property institution consistent with man's natural rights, an ambition in which he has been followed by more than one contemporary philosopher (Nozick, 1974; Steiner, 1977b). Again, Adam Smith evaluated some forms of property, and inheritance practices, by reference to their contribution to an efficient market. Letourneau denounced the excesses of individualism which produced inequality and threatened the maintenance of social harmony, while Marx identified private property with class society and anticipated the demise of both. Rights, needs, labouring capacities, divine injunction, efficiency, harmony, liberty and justice – however understood by particular authors – have been involved in these histories, and the continuing political issue of property is its compatibility with values like these.

There are obviously many ways in which discussion of the legitimacy of property could be organised. We might, for example, want to consider arguments for private property and arguments for common property; or we might distinguish rights-based theories from those with other premises. In the following chapters arguments are organised around a number of themes: the connections between liberty, power and property; between labour and property; and problems posed by the movement of time for theories of property. This division of the discussion cuts across the other classifications mentioned, and has the advantage that it enables us to explore different understandings of values like liberty or justice, or of the nature of labour, in their connection with property.

It will be evident that considerations relevant to these themes have already been mentioned in this chapter. The relation between creativity, labour and property is an important component of disputes about the interpretation of Genesis, which mentions both God's act of creation and the labour to which fallen man was condemned. Locke's theory gives the property of each in his person and labour a crucial role in differentiating individual property from the common gift. And Adam Smith's discussion moves between the value added by labour and the labourer's property in his work. Marx supported his argument for common property in the means of production with a conception of the social character of labour. So both historically and normatively, the connection between the expenditure of labour and the existence of property has been variously conceived. The theme is developed in Chapter 5.

Similar points may be made about the connection between property and power or liberty. In the Genesis story, was the grant made by God to Adam of property or power or both? In Smith's account, the form and distribution of property lead to or are associated with different principles of power and authority, and commercial society is valued because of the dependence otherwise produced by property holdings. Marx linked property in productive resources to the circumstances in which exploitation occurred. These are simply examples of a general concern about the relation between property, power and liberty which we shall explore in Chapter 4.

Finally, a third theme is concerned with the status of property with respect to the passage of time. The resources of this world outlast any particular generation (although, of course, some particular resources can be exhausted within a generation). Any account of the legitimacy of property must deal with this, balancing the claims of different generations to the resources available. Should we respect a division of property to which our forebears agreed, even though we were not consulted? Is inheritance a desirable practice? On what terms should inheritance be allowed? Should long possession ever give a person an entitlement to the resource possessed? All these questions relate to the differing time spans of natural persons, physical resources and legal entitlements. We shall explore them in Chapter 6.

4 Property, Liberty and Power

This chapter is concerned with the connections between property, power and liberty. This is an enormous subject, not only because 'property' is complex but also because there are different conceptions of liberty and power. A glance at the framework put forward in Chapter 2 will quickly reveal that each element in it could be variously specified in ways which would impinge on those different conceptions. It would certainly not be possible to advance any illuminating permutation of conceptions of liberty and *detailed* property systems, so we shall be extremely selective in this chapter.

Our initial problem is to separate in a useful way arguments about property, in its connection with liberty and power, from arguments about property in its connection with labour. In connection with property, the distinction between arguments about liberty and arguments about labour poses a problem in three different ways (cf. Ryan, 1983b). First, 'property' is central to a range of arguments about self-realisation, externalisation and individuation in which both liberty and labour are implicated. Hegel's theory provides an example (Teichgraeber, 1977). Secondly there are cases in which it is a matter of dispute whether the basic value advanced in an argument is liberty or the realisation of some aspect of creative personality. Here Marx's theory provides an example (Brenkert, 1980). Thirdly, some arguments about property which start from the expenditure of labour look reducible to arguments from liberty. Locke's theory provides an example, the more so since it embodies the language of rights. To assert a right is to assert a freedom with respect to something (Hart, 1955), so rights-based theories of property based on labour will always raise a problem about the relation between labour and liberty.

For at least these three reasons, separating 'liberty' from 'labour' in its connection with property is a hazardous procedure. Nevertheless, this chapter excludes arguments about self-realisation, rights-based arguments from labour expenditure, and those aspects of the Marxist theory which stress the species-character of labour which will be treated in Chapter 5.

Two classifications of the arguments about property and liberty suggest themselves. The first relies on a distinction between negative and positive liberty (Berlin, 1969), and asks what property regimes are consistent with those notions. The usual answer is that negative liberty is associated with private property, and positive liberty with common property. Although, as we shall see, such an association exists, it is certainly not a logical consequence of the conception of liberty alone. For example, Rousseau has a positive conception of liberty, but he seems to favour a reasonably equal distribution of private property in *The Social Contract* and state property in *The Constitution for Corsica* (1915, vol. 2, pp.302–3). Hobbes has a negative conception and favours limited private property (n.d. pp.136–45, p.213). On the other hand, Marx (e.g. 1977, p.92) argues for common property on the basis of a positive conception, while T. H. Green (1931, pp.1–27, pp.211–29), another positive libertarian, favours private property. We shall examine this issue later in this chapter.

A second alternative is to begin with private or common property, and to ask what implications for liberty (variously conceived) arise. But it is often too simple to ask whether common or private or state property is most conducive to freedom, first because the question of which agency holds the property is sometimes irrelevant to questions of liberty and secondly because we are not necessarily committed to a system of *exclusively* private or *exclusively* common property. We may take four illustrations of this point.

First, it is presumably uncontentious that slaves lack liberty. But slaves lack liberty whether the title to them rests with individuals or with the state, and historically there have been state-owned slaves (Finley, 1980). It is unlikely that an argument linking the extent of the slaves' unfreedom with the agency which owned them could be produced, at either a logical or empirical level.

Secondly, married women in nineteenth-century England suffered from an incapacity to own some kinds of property in their own names. The liberty of married women was certainly affected by those property rules. Clearly, the issue for liberty here is the distribution of legal powers. It is not a matter of private against public ownership, but of the balance between powers of different individuals. To live in a society in which private property plays a significant part, and to be denied the power to own it, is to suffer a lack of liberty. So here the issue is one of the appropriate distribution of legal power (J. S. Mill, 1983; H. T. Mill, 1983; Holcombe, 1983).

The more general version of this point refers to the nature of ownership. The content of ownership distributes freedoms between owners, and between owners and non-owners. For example, Honoré identified the incident of 'liability to execution' as part of the modern liberal concept of ownership. Liability to execution, as we saw, entails that the law may take property from a person, for example to pay his debts. Such an incident balances, as it were, the claims of different property owners. Again, the way in which ownership is treated balances the claims of an owner as against other persons. This operates in two ways. The more obvious is that an owner has powers to try to prevent others doing some things to or with his property. The less obvious is that rules about, for example, inheritance and alienability, balance the intensity of one person's ownership against that of other potential owners. All this has implications for liberty.

The third example of the irrelevance of questions of agency to liberty is provided by worries about the distribution of property itself, not merely legal powers over it. T. H. Green was disturbed lest the tendency of property to accumulate in a few hands led to the propertylessness (and hence lack of freedom, conceived of as the ability to pursue a rational plan of life) of some individuals. Here there might be room for arguments in favour of redistribution, rather than abolition, of private property; for amelioration of its effects, rather than its avoidance. The same case has been put in opposition to state property. It makes individuals dependent on the state. The worry about the distribution of property is not exclusively a matter of whose hands it is placed in.

Fourthly, and finally, there is a range of arguments which connect property and liberty both through the *form* of that property (as in the illustration of slavery) and through its *distribution* (as in the problem emphasised by T. H. Green). Here arguments about the means of production and the relationship between land and liberty

are examples. The question of the *form* of property is combined
with postulates about its *distribution*, which may be logical or
empirical. As we have seen, from accounts of the development of
property, the form which it adopts and the rules regulating its
transmission have been regarded as highly significant. Whether the
connection between property and liberty be pursued by analysing
the precise nature of Adam's dominion, or by looking at the
authority principle associated with particular forms of property, or
by looking at the connection between property and economic
surplus, a major concern has been with the connection between the
form of property and its *distribution*.

As these examples show, the problem of 'liberty' and 'property' is
not merely one of determining whether private or common
property is more conducive to freedom. For this reason, we shall
leave consideration of the general question of the relationship
between positive and negative liberty and property until the end of
the chapter. We shall first look at some issues which arise in relation
to particular forms of property, namely land and the means of
production, and issues which arise from the relationship of property
to institutions of the market and the state.

This discussion of land and the means of production is helpful for
four reasons. First, the initial element in our framework is 'items of
property', and these two 'items' enable us to illustrate the sorts of
issues that arise in particular cases. Secondly, land has been
historically very important, and some of the arguments connecting
property to liberty and power refer exclusively to it. Despite that,
thirdly, land is also a form of property used in production, so it
shares some features with all productive resources. Many of the
issues about property and power are concerned with the process of
production. Fourthly, attention to these arguments will enable us to
move on to look at property in relation to markets and subsequently
to address issues about the state. These explorations will enable us
to see why it is so difficult to connect particular conceptions of
liberty with particular property structures (Ryan, 1984b), a
problem pursued in the final section of the chapter.

Land and the means of production

English law, distinguished (and continues to distinguish) between real property and personal property. The rules regulating the transfer and transmission of these two forms of property were for centuries very different, and to some extent remain so. Real property, most obviously land, but also buildings and certain rights which may be construed as being 'attached' to land in some way, has some degree of geographical fixity. Because the rules governing these types of property differed, the way in which particular property was classified could be very important. We are told of a seventeenth-century case in which 'all the judges of England' were gathered together to decide whether dung was real property or personal property. It was held that 'a heap' was personal property, but 'dung spread on the land' was real property. Dung was, of course, an important economic asset and how it was classified determined whose hands it would come into when the owner died (Baker, 1971, pp.120–37, p.206).

In addition to the distinction between real property and personal property in the law, from which important consequences flowed, both ancient and modern political thought has attached particular significance to land. It is worth reviewing the different types of connections to which attention has been drawn not for property in general but for land in particular. The peculiar significance of what we may call real property was, according to Hannah Arendt, recognised by Greek and Roman notions: 'According to ancient understanding, man could liberate himself from necessity only through power over other men, and he could be free only if he owned a place, a home in the world' (1961, p.148). A precondition of independence from necessity was power over others, but this freedom was to be located in a particular sphere a man could call his own, the base from which his operations in the public world could be conducted (1961, p.253). Economic security and a place in the world flowed from ownership. Contemporary political rhetoric about 'property-owning democracy' draws on similar ideas.

Arguments about the particular significance of land are of two kinds: arguments that land is important in a specified respect, whatever other forms of property there are; and arguments that there is an historical decline in the importance of land, as other forms of property become in some way more prominent. One point which emerges clearly from attempts to characterise the historical development of property is concern with how earlier ideas about the significance of land were challenged by the realisation of the economic importance of mercantile or commercial property.

Land has one key position in relating individuals to the polity which is not dependent on what other forms of property happen to exist. Land provides the territorial dimension of the political unit. Modern states, at least, are defined in part by the legal jurisdiction which they claim over particular territory (e.g. Boyce, 1982, p.311). No doubt the legal jurisdiction is not precisely co-extensive with territory; persons not physically present in a state may still be subject to its laws, and some territory within the boundaries of a state, such as an Embassy, may have a peculiar status. But these details do not undermine the connections between jurisdiction, territory and the political unit in any serious way. Land mediates, in this sense, between political power and individuals subject to it. For this reason, arrangements governing property in land, which aggregatively constitutes territory, have always been of particular concern.

Beyond this general consideration, the distinguishing features of land, by contrast with other forms of property, have been thought to lie in its visibility, its fixity, and its security. The combination of these characteristics underlies the notion that landowners are particularly tied to the interests and welfare of society. Because the property is fixed, it cannot be removed; so the landowner has a greater interest in the degree to which the community flourishes than he would if his property were in (say) money. The contrast is between 'real' and 'mobile' property (Pocock, 1975, pp.387–92) or between 'agrarian' and 'mercantile' property (Pocock, 1976, p.141; 1979, *passim*). As Adam Smith pointed out:

> 'A merchant, it has been said very properly, is not necessarily a citizen of any particular country. It is in a great measure indifferent to him from what place he carries on his trade; and a very trifling disgust will make him remove his capital, and together with it all the industry which it supports, from one country to another. No part of it can be said to belong to any particular country, till it has been spread as it were over the face of that country, either in buildings, or in the lasting improvement of lands.' (1976, p.426)

Smith summarises a long-standing strain of the political thought of classical republicanism but his additional emphasis on improvement recalls the economic consequences of mobility of capital not 'tied into' a particular place by a connection with land or buildings. Hence the political question of the regulation of 'exports' of various kinds emerges: for example, in the nineteenth century, debates about the desirability of the export of machinery and of artisanal skill (Berg, 1980, pp.203–25), and in our own time debates about the regulation of powers to export capital by investing abroad.

For centuries the idea that only landowners had a sufficient interest to be entitled to share in political power was dominant. In the United Kingdom the Conservative enthusiasm for selling council houses and one argument for taxation relief on mortgage payments both depend on the view that the ownership of real property ties the interests of the individual owner to those of the broader community in a distinct way, to the benefit of political stability and, perhaps, economic activity.

It is obvious that land was the major economic resource before the development of commercial society. To say this does not entail any particular view of the dating of that development: the importance of trade and monetary wealth in classical times and in the Italian republics clearly pre-dates Adam Smith's analysis of commercial society in the eighteenth century. That land was a major economic resource, of course, provided one reason for its veneration and importance. Nevertheless, subsidiary elements of the same idea are worth mentioning. First, land has a greater security than many other forms of property. Although someone might eject me from my house, or from my land, thus temporarily denying me possession of it, he cannot carry it off as he can my wallet. Public knowledge about title (or at least the history of occupation) is greater in the case of real property. In addition, the physical property cannot be hidden or transported. If incentives for preserving and improving property depend upon the degree of security enjoyed in its possession – one of the most repeated arguments of all about property – then land possesses this quality to a greater degree than other forms (Smith, 1976, p.358, p.377, cf. p.423).

A second element is the connection between land and military power. If land is the major economic resource, then it is also the basis on which armies can be raised, so the question of who controls it has an obvious significance. A recent example is the decision by the Greek Supreme Court that aliens are debarred from owning land in frontier regions – an illustration that conjoins 'interest in the community' with 'military importance'. The two were often combined: not only is the ownership of land vital to the disposition of armies, but also those who own land have a particular interest in defending the community (they have something directly at stake, which cannot be removed, hidden etc.). An extension of this argument, historically, was the suggestion that not only did landowners have a particular interest in defending the political unit, but also that they had a particular capacity to do so, since their way of life suited them for military activity.

A further aspect of the fixity and security of land should also be noticed. Land is 'permanent', or at least it has some potentiality for permanence, and the supply of land is 'fixed': in that sense it is naturally scarce. Not surprisingly, therefore, problems of inheritance and justice between generations were raised about land at an early date. But in addition, the transmission of property through the generations is another way of tying individuals into the community through the agency of the family, both from the viewpoint of the heir whose land is subject to a particular jurisdiction and from that of the present owner, who might be alleged to have an interest and an incentive which transcends his own custody of the property. Land is a visible and tangible part of Burke's (1910, p.93) famous contract between generations, and the role of land in linking generations to a common way of life has been a recurrent theme. The notion that the present holders of (landed) property have responsibilities to their forebears and successors in their use and disposition of land relies on these features of fixity, security and permanence.

No doubt some of the arguments about the particular importance of land and its relation to power which we have been reviewing are less compelling when alternative sources of livelihood exist (but cf. Newby et al, 1978). Nevertheless, there is a fundamental case which connects liberty with property directly through land. This is the point that all action in which we are engaged has a spatial dimension. Herbert Spencer's argument, in the first edition of *Social Statics*, denied the legitimacy of private property in land, for this very reason. If persons had exclusive control over land, and if all land were owned, then anyone who did not own land could act, or perhaps even exist, only by permission of the landed. Hillel

Steiner (1982, pp.526–7) has described the following as the 'key passage' in Spencer's argument:

'Equity, therefore, does not permit property in land. For if *one* portion of the earth's surface may justly become the possession of an individual, and may be held by him for his sole use and benefit, as a thing to which he has an exclusive right, then *other* portions of the earth's surface may be so held; and eventually the *whole* of the earth's surface may be so held; and our planet may thus lapse altogether into private hands. Observe now the dilemma to which this leads. Supposing the entire habitable globe be so enclosed, it follows that if the landowners have a valid right to its surface, all who are not landowners, have no right at all to its surface. Hence, such can exist on the earth by sufferance only. They are all trespassers. Save by permission of the lords of the soil, they can have no room for the soles of their feet. Nay, should others think fit to deny them a resting-place, these landless men might equitably be expelled from the planet altogether. If, then, the assumption that land can be held as property involves that the whole globe may become the private domain of a part of its inhabitants; and if, by consequence, the rest of its inhabitants can then exercise their faculties – can then exist even – only by consent of the landowners; it is manifest, that an exclusive possession of the soil necessitates an infringement of the law of equal freedom. For, men who cannot "live and move and have their being" without the leave of others, cannot be equally free with those others.' (Spencer, 1851, pp.114–15)

If, for argument's sake, we allow that Spencer has demonstrated the existence of such a law, we may separate the assumptions upon which property in land will necessarily violate it. First, we should note the intensity of the ownership which is assumed: an owner has an exclusive right to a portion of the earth's surface, entailing that no-one else has any right whatsoever to it. But this is not how ownership is now understood, and it is doubtful whether Spencer's conclusion would follow so readily if the intensity of ownership were moderated. Secondly, the connection between the assumption that 'land can be held as property' and the conclusion that the whole planet belongs to only one part of the population could be construed as a logical possibility or an empirical likelihood. There is a distributional problem here of the kind we mentioned earlier, when we distinguished an argument from liberty against slavery (a *form* of property inimical to liberty) from hybrid cases (like property in the means of production or land) in which the argument from liberty may be contingently dependent on the *distribution* of property. Spencer's argument provides an example: it depends on a particular form of property, land, but it also relies on assumptions about distribution to draw its conclusion. To know whether Spencer's objection is to a *form* of property or to its *distribution* we should have to know whether the equal liberty principle would be satisfied if each person owned an equal share of the planet's surface. If the case in which each owned an equal share satisfies the equal liberty principle, then the argument is against a *maldistribution* of private property in land; but if such an equal distribution does not satisfy the principle (perhaps because of instability or the problem of subsequent generations) then the argument is against private property of a particular form. We shall see that similar ambiguities surround some arguments against private property in the means of production.

Spencer's fear that those who could (legitimately) be excluded from any soil could effectively be deprived of life may itself rest on a number of different notions. The connection between *legitimate* exclusion and mere exclusion is one to which we shall return. To be excluded from land would be to be excluded from the fruits of nature, and from the opportunity to produce with the aid of the soil. Gerrard Winstanley (1973, pp.120, 272, 382) disputed the legitimacy of private property in land for at least those two reasons, which serve as a bridge between arguments about the special nature of land and arguments about the means of production. For clearly, one might claim access to land because one has physical needs, or because one has a 'need' to expend labour. Although this second sort of need does not concern us directly here, the purchase of the two cases is somewhat different.

The argument against private property in the means of production has been variously formulated; and in these formulations one important difference is between those which set out from human needs and those which set out from productive activity. Marx argued that man has to produce to satisfy his needs; that his labour in this production constituted a species-distinct characteristic; that man needed to labour to be human and that the way in which the productive activity was pursued constituted a mode of production. Although we are not here concerned with arguments about property in relation to labour, one aspect of Marx's argument, and of much socialist thought (Furniss, 1978), does require attention: the claim that property in the means of production confers power on those who own it. ('Own' must be taken here to include 'control', although we have already seen that ownership and control may diverge (above, Chapter 2).)

If we distinguish labour from all else necessary to production, then clearly labour may stand in various different relations to those other 'things'. One person might possess, in addition to his labour, everything else necessary to produce – raw materials, tools, knowledge and so on. Or one person may possess some, but not all, of the 'things' needed. Marx's analysis of capitalism rests on the case in which one group of persons possess the capacity to labour, and nothing else, while another group owns the means of production. Propertyless labourers require access to the means of production in order to produce, and therefore to survive, and the terms on which that access is available advantage the owners of the means of production (Marx, 1977, pp.222–31). This simple case is a generalisation of that put by Spencer, who was concerned specifically with land. Spencer was concerned that those who privately owned land might exclude non-owners. The present argument suggests that those who own the means of production may exclude non-owners, or allow them access only on terms favourable to the owners. Just as Spencer's argument leaves unclear the connection between the form of property and its distribution, so many arguments about the means of production run together an overt concern with the form of property with other considerations, often without explaining the supposed connections between the two.

While it is true that some activity is necessary to satisfy a need, the activity and the need may be attributable to separate persons. My activity may satisfy both your need and mine, or yours but not mine; babies clearly have needs, but very little of the activity by which those needs are satisfied is their own. For this reason, it makes a considerable difference whether we begin from needs or from the expenditure of labour. Again, the activity which satisfies need is variously describable: whether we call it labour or productive activity depends on how these terms are construed. If we follow

Marx's apparent meaning of production, as a process of mastery of nature, then needs may be satisfied (in some circumstances) without production occurring. The mere use of nature, where no effort is made to control it, but only to employ its fruits, is presumably not production.

The stress on the means of *production* in theories of property can clearly arise from different sources, and the purchase of the arguments consequently varies. If the need-satisfaction is the starting point (e.g., men need access to land which produces food if they are not to starve) then the central question is how to make the satisfaction of need compatible with particular forms or distributions of property, and the level of need-satisfaction aimed at may be crucial to the answer. Alternatively, the starting point might be that man can be truly human only if engaged in productive activity. These arguments have different conclusions: in the first case, the argument against property in the means of production on the ground that it prevents the satisfaction of basic needs might be met by pointing to mechanisms alleged to take care of such satisfaction, for instance, the market or the welfare state. On the other hand, if needs are treated broadly, or the argument starts from the essential human characteristic of production, then the case against property in the means of production would still be running even if basic needs were satisfied. Hence such arguments seek to show either that property in the means of production inhibits output and that a better alternative can be specified, or that arrangements could be made by which everyone could engage in 'true' productive activity.

These different starting points for an argument against property in the means of production may be supplemented by an argument from a more specific notion of liberty. To the extent that someone lacks the means to produce (other than labour) that person necessarily depends on another. If liberty in the sense of independence is valued, then the lack of means of production inhibits independence. There are two different directions in which this argument can be taken. The first aims at a redistribution of productive resources, so that everybody has some. The second aims at provision of access to the means of production. The first is compatible with private property, and may indeed see its ownership as the basis of independence, while wishing to increase the number of independent persons. The second may be compatible with forms of private property or may go further to advocate its abolition, to guarantee the access with which it is concerned. 'Provision of access to the means of production' may thus conclude with relatively weak claims (the 'right to a job' or 'the right to work') or with relatively strong ones ('public ownership' of the means of production or 'nationalisation'). Socialist criticisms of private property in the means of production, and liberal criticisms of state socialism both point to the dependence the criticised system imposes, and proposals for market socialism attempt to avoid the perils of both (Miller, 1977; Goodin, 1982, p.92).

Obviously, the arguments which are here separated, partly to show that individually they have different possible conclusions, are often found together. Marx held that capitalism had increased the forces of production enormously, but did not necessarily produce what people 'really' wanted or ensure that they obtained it. The private ownership of capital also enabled the extraction of surplus value, prevented the worker having any choice about his productive activity, and inhibited the development of persons by the division of labour which it imposed. Which of these conditions is the basis of any theory of exploitation in Marx's writings is the subject of some dispute (Cohen, 1980; Brenkert, 1980; Buchanan, 1982; Holstrom, 1977). But that all these arguments are contained in Marx's criticism of capitalism does not entail that they have to be treated as a set, and many socialists have been selective about them. For example, early twentieth-century British socialists advocated nationalisation or public ownership largely on grounds of productive efficiency (construed to include reducing unemployment) and of liberty (construed to include both the absence of poverty and the presence of choice in working activity) (Pelling, 1954, pp.291–308).

The question so far evaded, however, is 'what are the means of production?' For example, the Webbs wrote:

'. . . what is referred to as instruments of production is not, pedantically, every tool or accessory by which production is assisted – there is no suggestion that a carpenter should not individually own his kit of tools, the seamstress her needle, or the clerk his fountain pen – but merely what is commonly included by the business man as capital, such as is provided by a joint-stock company engaged in manufacture or commerce.' (Pelling, 1954, p.297)

This quotation, incidentally, illustrates the point made above; for to argue against a form of property, that it produces dependence, is compatible with recognising that the same property in other hands produces independence. But what is confused, here, is a case which starts from the type of property, (the so-called instruments of production) with a case which starts from some other aspect of the pattern of resources. In other words, if the objection is not to property in the means or instruments of production, but some persons' property in those instruments, the argument would be better setting out from the objectionable feature. In this case it is presumably either the concentration of the means of production or ownership of capital by non-workers which is taken to be a problem. One approach is therefore to isolate property which is thought to have coercive potential.

The discussion of the form of property (e.g. instruments of production) can become entangled with arguments about its distribution (e.g. large holdings) through a proposition that logically or empirically a particular type or property or even property in general becomes concentrated in a few hands. Disputes about property and liberty are therefore often caused by disagreement over the way in which markets operate, over the connection between the form of property and its distribution. Green (1931, p.220) was worried that there might be a contradiction between the rationale of property ('everyone should be secured by society in the power of getting and keeping the means of realising a will, which in possibility is a will directed to the special good'), on one side, and freedom of bequest and trade on the other.

He admitted that '. . . if an inequality of fortunes, of the kind which naturally arises from the admission of these two forms of freedom, necessarily results in the existence of a proletariate, practically excluded from such ownership as is needed to moralise a man, there would be a contradiction between our theory of the right of property and the actual consequence of admitting the right according to the theory' (1931, p.221). Green's worry is about propertylessness, entailing a restriction on the pursuit of the moral life; Marx's analysis of propertylessness was part of his explanation of the extractive potential of capital. Green was worried about the consequences of freedom of trade, in general; Marx was particularly concerned with production. Green's disquiet was compatible with a conclusion advocating moderation of the powers of owners (particularly with respect to bequest), while Marx advocated the abolition of private property in the means of production.

The initial concern in discussions of the special importance of property in the means of production, then, is with the terms on which persons can gain access to them. This applies both to socialist arguments about the power which the capitalist class acquires by virtue of its private ownership of those means, and to anti-socialist arguments which draw attention to the equivalent danger when the property is in the hands of the state. But the attempt to draw the connection between property and power will require attention to the size and distribution of holdings, as well as their overt form, and thus leads on to dispute both about the operation of markets and the implications of inequality for liberty.

Two problems arise when we attempt to define the means of production. First, should we include only those resources actually used in production, or also those that might be? A private house is not a means of production in a narrow sense, but becomes one if a productive activity is carried on within it. The arguments we have reviewed would be as applicable to 'potential' means of production as to existing ones: this is particularly true of the view that private ownership limits the satisfaction of needs, a view forcibly expressed by Gerrard Winstanley (1973, p.272).

All arguments against private property in the means of production will have some application to property in *potential* means of production. For example, if the argument is that such property confers power on its owners, because they can determine the conditions under which labour achieves access, then holding a resource which could be used in production, but is not, amounts to total exclusion. So if the property rules allow private property in the means of production, opposition to such arrangements may be logically extended to a great deal of property. The solution has usually been to invoke another consideration – such as the extent of concentration – to define the cut-off point. It is worth noticing that for those systems which require the means of production to be state property the definitional problem is easier, but the conceptual connection still exists. If the property rules require that the state owns the means of production, then anything *in fact* used in production has to be treated as state property. An argument which maintained that state property made individuals dependent upon the state, even if *potential* means of production were not state property, could not be refuted by pointing to those resources, since, were they to be applied to production, their status would necessarily change.

A second problem in the definition of 'means of production' arises from co-operation. If we treat the means of production as that with which labour needs to co-operate in order to produce, we face a difficulty about skill, knowledge and expertise. If these may be taken to be part of labour itself, the means of production have a tangible character; but if they may not be so taken, the denial of private property in the means of production has very broad implications. For example, a musical score seems straightforwardly to be the product of the composer, and thus a product of his or her labour – this builds skill, expertise and talent into 'labour' itself. From the point of view of the potential performer, however, the product of the composer's labour is a means of production. So if the objection is to private property in the means of production, the question arises: are these to be defined from the viewpoint of the potential producer, or from the viewpoint of someone creating something which may be someone else's means of production? The argument against the composer's copyright is that the score is the musician's means of production. But if the score is the musician's means of production, so is the composer's labour, because if the musician cannot perform without the *product* of the composer's labour, *a fortiori* he cannot perform without the composer's labour. So denial of property in the means of production, strictly construed, has broad implications.

It may be objected that this argument presupposes individual labour, and looks at the distinction between labour and means of production in the wrong way. The distinction, it might be replied, is not between one person's labour and that which he needs to produce, but between social labour and what society needs to produce. To put the distinction in this way is to stress the social character of labour, and the implications of such an argument for property must be discussed separately in Chapter 5. It is sufficient to note here one argument against private property in the means of production which flows from an attachment to a specific notion of liberty. This 'liberty' is conceived to include choice-making in the productive process, best realised by 'common' property.

If this is to be individual rather than collective choice, then the case that private property in the means of production inhibits this liberty would equally apply to others' choices about their labour expenditure. To achieve equal liberty, in the specific sense of equal capacity to direct one's production, may then require social choices about the labour of all. The liberty of each to choose his productive activity and equal choice of productive activity may be impossible to reconcile except through collective decision making – about either common property or agreed constraints on private property.

The connection between property in the means of production and liberty may, then, be drawn in several different ways. First, there is the view that property in the means of production confers power on the 'owners' at the expense of the propertyless, and keeps them in (relative) poverty. This may be unpacked into a claim for a (greater) share of output or into a claim for direct access to the means to produce. Secondly, there is the view that property in the means of production confers power on its owners at the expense of others by limiting freedom of choice in productive activity. This may be unpacked into the claim that individuals should be able to exercise that capacity with respect to their own case, or into the claim that collectively individuals should exercise it with respect to all. Thirdly, there is the view that, while property in the means of production *as such* may be innocuous, concentrations of this sort of property have one or more of the undesirable features already mentioned. The preferred explanation of the concentration is then crucial: is it a logical consequence of the nature of the property or a contingent empirical characteristic of some property holding? These three views may each lead to a desire to redistribute property or to abolish it; and as formulated in this summary may be applied to both private and state property in the means of production (cf. Freymond, 1962).

For this reason, although the dispute between proponents of state or common property and advocates of private property is often represented as resting upon different conceptions of freedom, it is clear that persons with the same conception could come to different conclusions about desirable property arrangements because they disagreed about the empirical or logical characteristics of an economic system. T. H. Green was held back from the conclusion drawn by Marx because he thought that the tendency of property to accumulate in a few hands could be avoided or at least moderated (1931, p.225). The focus of the argument is usually the connection between property rules and the distribution of property, so it is not surprising that writers with different ideas about liberty – for example, James Harrington (Reeve, 1984), Adam Smith, J. S. Mill (1865, pp.123–45) and T. H. Green (1931, pp.211–29) – have been led to examine closely alienability and hereditability. These two aspects of the property rules constitute a nexus between forms of property and its distribution.

Property, the market and capitalism

Because critics of private property have often been critics of 'the market' or of 'capitalism' as well, it is not always easy to isolate the specific characteristics of private property to which exception is taken. We encountered aspects of this difficulty in the previous discussion of the means of production, in which we discovered that distribution, form, size of holdings as well as assumptions or arguments about the operation of markets were intertwined. For this reason, it is worth trying to isolate the conceptual connections between property, the market and capitalism.

'Capitalism' is a form of market operation; it is one way in which markets may be organised. There is no necessary identity between criticism of capitalism and the rejection of all markets. Some critics of capitalism seem to have envisaged the possibility of a society of independent producers connected by market institutions (e.g. Hodgskin, 1832). The system of market socialism has been advocated as a solution to some of the 'undesirable' features of both capitalism and socialism (Miller, 1977). One could reject capitalism as a system, yet favour the operation of markets; but the operation of a market is dependent on the existence of some form of private property. Agreement on the conceptual connection between markets and private property is consistent with both rejection of such property and support for it, depending on the evaluation of the complete market system.

'A market' is a forum for exchange. Either goods or services may be exchanged; exchange may be direct or mediated by money. Some markets are very sophisticated – for example, futures markets, or markets involving contingent products. In general, a market system may be more or less extensive along two dimensions: first, types of market are distinguished by the number of buyers and sellers – monopoly, monopsony etc. Secondly, the range of goods and services allocated by the market may be a more or less extensive proportion of the total produced or made available. The market is a distributional device – one way in which it is 'decided' who gets what. The usual claim is that this 'decision' is in some specific respect better made by the market than by any other procedure, such as allocation of shares by an individual decision-maker. The market is also treated as a process, because to say that the market 'decides' may be misleading for two reasons. First, it assumes an end-point which may not exist. Secondly, the results of the interactions are not under anyone's control, and the market is not 'deciding' as an individual does.

The notion that results are not under anyone's control, however, depends on the extent of the market in the first of the two senses identified above. A monopolist can control the price at which goods are sold (though a profit-maximising monopolist cannot control both price and quantity sold). In a perfect market, this degree of control is unavailable. A 'perfect' market, however, is a theoretical construct. In its purest form it assumes, *inter alia*, absence of transactions costs and perfect information. It is vital in discussing markets to distinguish claims about the consequences of perfect market operation from claims about actual market operation; and to separate both from dispute about the extent to which any possible market could meet the specified conditions.

The general characterisation of a market, then, is a device by which goods and services are distributed to persons by the operation of a price mechanism which allows buyers and sellers to respond to other persons without any particular knowledge of each other. A 'market system' is usually intended to denote an economic structure with an extensive set of particular markets. To what extent does a market system depend upon a particular property system?

In the simple model of bartering, two individuals exchange goods because both have a want for that which the other possesses. Even such a simple system of mutual exchange relies on some excludability, whether *de facto* or *de jure*, for no-one would be inclined to give something up to acquire something else if he could obtain it by force or right. If the exchange is conceived as occurring before settled law, then the basis of exclusion must be physical or conventional; after effective law has been established, of course, it is a matter of enforced property rules. So a minimum pre-supposition of exchange is that persons have either the ability or the right to exclude the other partner in the exchange from the 'property'. Since such an exchange is the most basic form of market transaction imaginable, it follows that markets presuppose some excludability.

This straightforward idea may be developed in different directions. First, the desirable set of property rights may be specified by reference to the outcomes generated by a market, by arguing both that a market system is ideal and that a particular set of property rights allows an actual market to function in a way which more clearly approximates that ideal than another set. The linkage between property and the market is clear and direct, and the justification for the content of property rules is indirect or instrumental. It is indirect, because the justification for the property rules is carried on the back of the justification for the market system (see generally Furubotn and Pejovich (1972); for a specific example, Brittan, 1977, pp.209–17).

Nevertheless, in a world in which markets are not perfect, this approach can raise interesting problems of the 'second best'. Imperfect markets do not produce all the desirable features of ideal markets, and the imperfections are not necessarily due to badly defined property rules. Where such imperfections exist, it may well be better (on the same criteria which underpin the preference for a market) to deviate from the property rules suggested by the ideal market model. This problem is recognised by defenders of the role of private property in the market system, like Hayek (1982, vol 1, pp.108–9).

A second direction in which the simple exchange model may be developed is, as it were, backward rather than forward. Whereas one view of the justification and desirability of property rules flows from their status in relation to a market order, this second view looks back from those holdings to ask how they could have arisen. The holdings which are taken for granted on the first view are the outcome of a process deserving investigation on the second. After all, it might be agreed that *if* individuals had exclusive control over objects and *if* a market order were in operation the claimed consequences would follow; but it might yet be objected that such exclusive control could never have arisen legitimately, so the consequential story is irrelevant to the justification of property. James Buchanan has combined the consequentialist story with an account of the 'origins' of property. Buchanan's theoretical enterprise begins with a natural distribution, in which the marginal costs in defence of holdings and of attack on others' holdings are equal to the marginal benefits of those activities. Buchanan uses the actors' forward-looking appreciation of the advantages of trade to suggest some sort of conventional acceptance of this natural distribution. *The Limits of Liberty* radically reformulates the traditional normative problem of property. Instead of starting with a conception of persons, and working to a set of property rules thought to be congruent with it, Buchanan (1975, p.10) believes that the delineation of property rights (the conventional acceptance of the 'natural' distribution) discloses a definition of the human agent.

Of course, not all defenders of the market order are interested in the question of the origins of property. This is partly because the market order is treated as a rule-governed process, in which to talk of starting points and end points is arbitrary. It is no accident that both Nozick (1974, pp.149–74) and Hayek (1982, vol. 2, pp.62–100) are antipathetic to notions of social justice which look at a distribution of resources at a particular point in the process of exchange. The difference between those authors in the present context, however, is that Nozick is prepared to mount a theory of original just acquisition while Hayek takes property as historically given or, at least, he takes long experience of private property as historically given, rejecting primitive communism as a socialist myth (1982, vol. 1, p.108).

The sceptical view, which generates an antipathy to private property from opposition to either capitalism in particular or the market in general, does not deny the conceptual connection between exclusive property and the operation of markets. It proceeds either by denying the value of the market system itself, or by pointing to features of the market system which the simple model we have been discussing ignores. These are first, that power relations are involved in the exchange, and that property is part of the explanation of that power; and/or, secondly, that the power which exists in this exchange or market sphere is translated into political power. So two clear issues emerge: first, does property confer power in the market and limit freedom (and if so, on what understanding of freedom)?; secondly, is market power translated into political power, and if so, what part does property play in the process?

We have already looked at some relevant arguments about liberty and property in our discussion about land and the means of production. The more particular focus of the present discussion is 'exchange'. A market system is one in which exchanges occur, and property is both something which may be exchanged and, in its distribution, a condition under which exchange occurs. For example, I may be selling fruit. The exchange transaction transfers fruit which is my property to you, and in return I receive money, which has hitherto been yours. But this transaction does not take place in a vacuum. A contested question surrounds the connection between the circumstances in which the transaction occurs – including the pre-existing distribution of resources – and the *content* of the transaction. A full treatment of this problem would require analysis of the exchange theory of power and the concept of exploitation (Lively, 1976; Roemer, 1982).

Clearly inequalities in holdings – among other inequalities, like differences in talents – will provide a *motive* for exchange. For example, I possess the apples which you lack. But power in an exchange can arise from these inequalities – for example, if I own all the orchards in the world, my monopoly power will be reflected in the price the market will bear. This does not mean that an exchange under such conditions cannot be mutually beneficial, only that the distribution of benefit will be different from that which would be obtained in an ideal market. Both supporters and opponents of the market could agree with these observations, but dispute the empirical characteristics of actual markets, or the extent to which such markets can ever approach the ideal case. Alternatively, supporters of the market may deny that the sorts of inequalities under discussion give rise to *power* in exchange, except perhaps in the limiting case in which one party has literally no choice but to enter into it. (Compare Nozick's treatment of a monopoly in water-wells and of the unique invention of a miracle drug (1974, pp.180–1).)

An example of the issue may be taken from theories of a 'just price'. According to some writers, a distinction could be drawn between a just price and one which exploited the buyer. For example, if there were a food shortage because of a bad harvest, prices would tend to rise. But would it be just to charge a price which yielded the farmer a return far in excess of what he received in a 'normal' year? Early writers had great doubts, but much of modern economics regards the attempt to determine a just price as mistaken, on the ground that what is just must be a matter of what individuals are prepared to pay in a market. This is not to deny that modern economics takes an interest in the 'abnormal' profit earned by a monopolist, for example; but there is an obvious difference between the explanatory concern of that modern interest and the ethical focus of theories of a just price. What is common, despite this difference, is reference to a base line. The abnormal profit of the monopolist, which is to be explained, is abnormal by reference to the situation in a (more) perfect market. Similarly, the unjust price is one which reflects a bad harvest, by reference to an average year, or one which reflects the dire need of the buyer, by reference to 'usual' conditions.

The relevance of these base-line conditions to theories of property in the present context is this. First, the exactions of a monopolist are undesirable both for defenders and opponents of the market (Elster, 1978). Their difference lies usually in the opponent's claim that monopoly is an inherent tendency in markets, or, less generally, is logically or empirically related to certain forms of property, like means of production. This is a question about the nature of the equilibrium markets. But a consistent free marketeer might well support regulation of property and its distribution on the same ground that an opponent deplored the market system – the undesirable features of monopoly. Secondly, need is the most traditional ground upon which property rules may legitimately be ignored. Hobbes (n.d., pp.196–7) and Grotius (1853, vol. 2, p.238), for example, recognised that taking what was another's, in conditions of dire need, and subject to safeguards, was legitimate. Their argument was less that need provided an excuse, than that need took away the character of a crime. Thirdly, the base-line conditions may include an alternative set of property rules. That is, what is criticised is a feature which if the property rules were different, would not exist. Historically this sort of argument has been pursued most vigorously with respect to the effect of markets on the level and distribution of output, and on the conditions of remuneration for labour.

We may distinguish these disputes about the operation of markets, and the place of property in market transactions, from disputes about property under capitalism. Although capitalism is a market system, and is therefore the subject of the controversies already mentioned, critics of capitalism have usually specified additional features of that system in addition to its market base. Capitalism includes a market system, but not all market systems are capitalist. What, then, are these additional features?

Marx insisted on two: that capitalism is a system of commodity production and that it depends on wage-labour. A commodity is something produced directly for exchange. So while a market is one of the means by which exchange occurs, a capitalist commodity system is one in which production is carried on in order to exchange the product. Because of the empirical dependence of this system on wage-labour, capitalism changes the form of private property: 'Self-earned private property, that is based, so to say, on the fusing together of the isolated, independent-labouring individual with the conditions of his labour, is supplanted by capitalistic private property, which rests on exploitation of the nominally free labour of others, i.e., on wage-labour' (Marx, 1974, p.714).

Four points may be made about this quotation. First, Marx is directing attention at the historical process by which labourers were separated from the means of production as capitalism developed. The importance of the 'means of production' has been discussed above. Secondly, it is clear that the economic system organised on the basis of 'independent-labouring' producers was a market system which depended upon private property but was not capitalist. Thirdly, this quotation occurs in a chapter in which Marx argues that 'the historical tendency of capitalist accumulation' is towards concentration of capital, which illustrates the possible connection between the *form* of property and its *distribution* discussed earlier. Fourthly, the circumstances of exploitation of 'nominally free labour' may be understood in various ways, some of which we have already encountered. In particular, it hints that despite the apparent freedom of labour, the labourer may not be truly free under a system of wage-labour based on private property. It is important to see that this conception of the particular importance of private property under capitalism may be shared by those who wish, with Marx, to replace it by some form of social ownership of productive resources, and by those who wish instead for a system which embodies 'self-earned private property'. The Webbs, we recall, saw no objection to the individual worker's property in his tools, but advocated the nationalisation of concentrations of capital.

Property, power and the state

Such a critique of capitalism takes us beyond the level of analysis with which we have so far dealt. On certain assumptions about interests, or class interests, there may be a difference between the analysis of an individual transaction and the analysis of a group of transactions. For example, Brian Barry (1980, p.344) has endorsed the notion that it makes conceptual sense to argue that *individual* capitalists are powerless, while the capitalist *class* is powerful. G. A. Cohen (1979, p.24) has argued that capitalism may not limit the freedom of any one proletarian, but nevertheless enslaves the proletariat. Our discussion of land and the means of production, of markets and capitalism, has enabled us to isolate some of the contentious questions surrounding the connection between property, power and liberty. But we still have to address another area in which property is regarded quite differently by theorists, namely its relation to political power and state activity. For simplicity, we may contrast a liberal pluralist attachment to private property with a Marxist dismissal of it, but we must recognise that both 'pluralist' and 'Marxist' positions come in many forms, and that this summary runs together positions which may be given varying emphases by various writers.

'Pluralism' is employed in many different senses. Against the anarchist, a pluralist holds that the state is necessary; against the Hobbesian he argues that the state need not be all-powerful. He pictures state power as necessary (to restrain) but dangerous (because liable to abuse and expansion). He further holds that state power is in principle neutral between competing interests. Different thinkers have made this account more or less coherent – often, it has been pointed out (Lively, 1978), a tension appears between the idea that the state is necessary and the idea that it can behave in a neutral fashion. The pluralist wishes to minimise restrictions on individuals, while denying the possibility of the anarchist ambition of dispensing with the state. Especially important, in the present context, is the pluralist denial of the Marxist theory of the state – in particular the claim that political power is more or less disguised class power. The pluralist concern with property reflects these various considerations.

Liberal pluralists think of the private property system as a limitation on the state in several ways. First, some have thought of property as pre-political, either in the sense that property exists in a 'state of nature' or in the sense that a right to property is a constitutional limitation on legitimate state activity. The former version envisages some general respect for others' holdings without coercive power, but a respect insufficiently general to negate the need for a state. The latter asserts a right to property to protect the individual's sphere from encroachment by the government, to assist in the definition of 'the private'. This private realm is a sphere of individual freedom, of which the right to private property is an essential ingredient. This does not, of course, mean that the extent of liberty is wholly governed by the private sphere defined by property rights. The right to property is valued because it restricts legitimate interference with individuals – they may not be divested of their property without consent, or proper cause (however defined), without compensation and so on.

A second reason for the pluralist attachment to private property arises from a consideration we addressed in the last section. Private property is a pre-condition of the market, and a pluralist concerned to keep state power in check has reasons for valuing the market system. The most important is that the market is held to recognise, or allow for, individual freedom because of the place it gives to individual choice. A second reason is that the market acts as a co-ordination device, providing an alternative to centrally-directed decision making which is held to limit freedom. The pluralist wishing to limit the power of the state associates its power with the functions it is called upon to perform, and thus seeks to limit those functions; this is also evident in the pluralist attachment to voluntary associations. If private property is a pre-condition of the market, and if the market provides an alternative to state activity, then the pluralist has an instrumental reason for valuing private property.

To the extent that liberal pluralism has been concerned with individuality, it has integrated an Aristotelian claim into consideration of property. Aristotle (1962, pp.62–4; Mathie, 1978) pointed out that common property is liable to neglect, since no-one feels the same responsibility for it as he does his own property. Those who have valued individuality have usually insisted that its development requires that the individual take responsibility for his own affairs. Private property enables an individual to take such responsibility and to express or assert his individuality. This is relevant to the relation between individuals and the state, because the pluralist wishes to minimise coercion while maintaining social order. One mechanism to pursue that aim is to ensure that individuals find it in their interest to do what they would otherwise have to be coerced to do. If common property is liable to neglect or abuse, then coercion may be necessary to ensure that individuals play their part in looking after it (Olson, 1965, pp.60–5). Where the property is private, the individual is thought to have an interest in looking after it himself. (The owner may nevertheless be legally constrained *if* he neglects his property.) Hence private property is thought to minimise the amount of necessary coercion, while common property is associated with authoritarian devices. A variant on this position was put forward by the so-called early English pluralists, who valued voluntary associations because they too restricted the functions the state was called upon to perform and because they offered the individual various spheres in which he could develop his personality. But such voluntary associations would themselves often require resources with which to pursue their common purposes, and thus these groups would have control over property. The recognition of the legal personality of such groups was advocated as a means of encouraging both their responsibility for their actions and the civic attachments of their members (Nicholls, 1975; for recent discussion, Manley, 1983).

We have already seen, in our brief discussion of Marx's historical treatment of property and modes of production, that 'private' property is associated by him with class societies. We know too, that despite the doubtful case of the Asiatic mode of production, the state in Marx's theory is a feature of class societies. In future society, private property, classes and the state will disappear. In capitalist society, the two great classes are the bourgeoisie and the proletariat, and the expectation is that the struggle between them will intensify as other groups are more and more absorbed into one of those classes. The state in capitalist society works in the interests of the capitalist class, which translates its economic dominance into political dominance. We have already looked at the arguments which attribute power to the capitalist class because of their relationship to the means of production, and we have looked at the way in which property is implicated in that analysis. Our present task is to determine the role allotted to property in the alleged convergence of economic and political power.

Political power was defined by Marx as class power used by one class to subordinate others. Miliband summarises one version of the analysis of the state as follows: 'In the Marxist scheme, the "ruling class" of capitalist society is that class which owns and controls the means of production and which is able, by virtue of the economic power thus conferred upon it, to use the state as its instrument for the domination of society' (1969, p.23).

The property of the capitalist class is held to enable that class to dominate society, and thus the other classes. But the mechanism by which this economic power becomes political power is unclear, and extremely controversial. In some versions, property is very directly involved. For example, it has been suggested that the bourgeoisie achieves control through its ownership of the national debt (Maguire, 1978, pp.18–19). In other versions, property is less central to the linkage. For example, it has been claimed that the state is constrained by capitalism and so cannot act in a way incompatible with it (Jessop, 1982). Although the precise role of property may be unclear, it is certainly implicated in the Marxist analysis of state power as class power. The relation between political power and property is therefore seen quite differently by Marxists and pluralists. At bottom, Marxists wish to abolish private property (of some kinds) because it provides economic and political power which bears coercively on individuals and inhibits their development. Pluralists, by contrast, see in private property a defence against or limitation of state power, a condition of freedom from the state and of individuality. Marxists see in property the potential for concentrated class power, pluralists see in it the means by which liberty may be diffused.

Finally, in looking at the connection between property, liberty and the state, we must glance at some problems which have arisen for democratic theory. This basic but abiding contrast between two particular positions does not, of course, explore the full range of thinking about the role of property in the power structure of a society or state. Nevertheless, the basic contrast still underlies debates between modern pluralists and Marxists and the anarchist tradition draws on both perspectives. Communitarian anarchists share the Marxists' dismay at the power conferred by property, while individualist anarchists hope to find freedom in a private-property market system (Miller, 1984, pp.30–59).

We have already met, in the discussion of land, the notion that representation should be restricted to those who have a fixed interest. A problem for advocates of an extension of the franchise has been to counter the argument that such an extension would undermine the security of property (Lively and Rees, 1978, pp.35–48). The extension of the suffrage, it was asserted, would lead to legalised redistribution, or to appropriation of property by the poor. Security of property required, therefore, restricting the vote to the propertied. This is not quite the same argument as that from the fixed interest, but clearly the two are liable to be used together. Both in the Putney debates (Woodhouse, 1974, pp.55–7), during the English Civil War, and in nineteenth-century discussion (Hansard, 1822, pp.109–11; 1823, p.1269), the vote itself was treated by some as being property, in the first case because the extension of the franchise was regarded as taking away property in the double sense of extending a privilege and enabling legalised redistribution, in the second case because the vote had an economic value to its possessor. This concern to reconcile a broad suffrage with security of property is part of a wider debate about how constitutional guarantees of such security can be made to work.

Liberty and property

We saw in the introduction to this chapter that the connections between liberty and property are complex, because both are capable of many specifications. Even a simple conjunction between negative and positive liberty on the one side and private and common property on the other does not produce any simple alignment of views. Not all negative libertarians have an unqualified enthusiasm for private property, and not all positive libertarians favour common property. In the last three sections we have looked at land and the means of production and at markets and the state, and this has enabled us to bring out some of the reasons why the same variant of property can be favoured by writers with different conceptions of liberty, while the same aspects of property are the focus for quite different arguments about liberty and power.

In this final section we shall look again at the implications of a commitment to a particular conception of liberty in the light of the previous discussion. It will be helpful to distinguish two understandings of negative liberty. Those who subscribe to the view that 'An individual is unfree only if his action is prevented by the action of another agent' (cf. Steiner, 1975, p.33) we shall call 'pure' negative libertarians. A 'moderate' negative libertarian believes that an individual's liberty is restricted by the interference of others. A moderate negative libertarian might include among such restrictions not only 'being prevented' but also 'being threatened' or 'hindered' in various other ways. The precise range of interferences by which negative liberty is reduced is a controversial matter (Berlin, 1969, pp.122–4). The positive libertarian, by contrast, is more directly concerned with freedom to *do* something, and not merely with the freedom from interference (Berlin, 1969, pp.130–2). So, for example, a positive libertarian may conclude that poverty reduces the liberty of the poor, a position denied by most negative libertarians whose conception of liberty as the absence of interference by others is not engaged by a particular distribution of resources. For this reason, a concern with negative liberty has been *associated* with liberalism and the acceptance of markets, while positive liberty has been *associated* with critiques of the market. For example, Raymond Plant has suggested that: 'A negative view of freedom is central to the liberal tradition of political thought and underpins the liberal conception of political and economic freedom as well as their critique of socialist views of liberty. Any attempt to secure positive rights to resources, to income, to work, to welfare are bound to be coercive and to violate basic negative rights, which include my right not to have my property taken away if I acquired it legally and non-coercively' (1984b, p.6). Despite this, we should not conclude that all negative libertarians are enthusiastic advocates of market systems, still less of capitalism. Even if we acknowlege an association between negative liberty and attachment to private property, we should certainly not regard the connection between the two as either universal or as a matter of logical entailment. To pursue this point we may invoke our distinction between pure and moderate negative libertarians.

As we saw in Chapter 2, property rules define various sorts of legitimate uses of resources, and various sorts of legitimate and illegitimate interferences with other persons. The *legitimacy* of such interferences is only contingently related to the prevention of action by others, with which the pure negative libertarian is concerned. This contingency arises in two ways. First, my prevention of your action may involve an illegitimate use of my property, but it is nonetheless prevention for that reason. For example, I might lock you in my house against your will. Secondly, even if I am entitled to use my property to prevent you from taking some action, I will not necessarily do so. For example, I may be allowed to build a wall round my land to exclude you, to prevent you from walking across it. I may, however, choose to allow you to take a short-cut.

This contingent connection recalls Spencer's argument about private property in land. His concern was that if such property were allowed, some persons might *equitably* be excluded from the planet altogether. A pure negative libertarian is not interested in what might equitably happen, but in what as a matter of fact does happen: is an agent prevented from doing *x* by others or not? So a pure negative libertarian will not see property rules *as such* reducing liberty, any more than he sees the law in general, which threatens sanctions on prohibited behaviour, as reducing liberty. Liberty is reduced only when property is used to prevent action, just as it is reduced only when the law carries out its threat (cf. Steiner, 1975, p.44; Oppenheim, 1981, pp.53–81). Because property rules are primarily about the legitimate use of resources, while pure negative liberty is about physically prevented action, and since legitimate use is only contingently related to prevented action, it seems that a pure negative libertarian will not be able to say anything much about the effect of property rules on liberty.

In one way this is not true of proponents of positive liberty. As we have seen, positive libertarians do not share a common prescription about desirable property rules, since, for example, Rousseau, T. H. Green and Marx are all positive libertarians but have different prescriptions about property. Nevertheless, for those who construe liberty as 'autonomy' or 'independence' the issue is reasonably clear, and we have encountered it in our discussion of the conceptual difficulties involved in talking about the means of production. On the one side, private property is seen as securing independence from others (the carpenter is to be allowed his tools), but on the other private property is implicated in reducing the independence of others (concentrations of capital diminish the capacity of the proletariat to lead a planned life). Part of 'autonomy', however, may be 'self-realisation' and the implications of an attachment to that goal are discussed in Chapter 5.

The difference between those who move from this recognition of the role of property in securing independence, while in some cases also threatening it, to advocacy of common property on one side or private property on the other, is partly a matter of how economic forces are understood to work. Marx emphasised the tendency of capital to concentration and the propertylessness of the proletariat. T. H. Green thought any such tendency could be sufficiently moderated by distributional devices. What is also at stake, however, is different assessments of the 'autonomy' or self-government enjoyed by persons under the two property regimes. Is collective decision-making about the lives of all an adequate or optimal realisation of the autonomy of each, or can such autonomy be better secured through a private property system, perhaps with distributional constraints? We have already discussed an aspect of this problem in exploring the 'means of production'. From the point of view of any one labourer, the labour of others is a means of *his* production, and for each to control his productive activity may then require that all decide about the activity of all. This is Rousseau's (1915, vol. 2, pp.42–6) prescription about law applied to collective control of productive resources, an extension only partly accepted by Rousseau. Marx embraced the idea, but in a very optimistic mood once supposed that each would be able to constantly choose his position in the social division of labour (1977, pp.169, 190–1).

A 'pure' negative libertarian, then, has to face the contingency of the connection between property and liberty on his definition. A positive libertarian has to explain his understanding of the relationship between self-government, autonomy, or independence and property. A moderate negative libertarian accepts that interference or restrictions on an agent, including being prevented from taking an action, are restrictions on freedom. One category excluded by the pure negative libertarian but included by moderate negative libertarians is punishability. A moderate accepts that if the law threatens punishment for performing a forbidden act, then liberty is reduced: this the purist denies, because no action is thereby prevented. Now property is enmeshed in a set of rules, and as we saw in Chapter 2 these rules are concerned with the rights, duties, liabilities and powers of those subject to them. A moderate negative libertarian is prepared to accept a range of interferences as reductions in freedom, and since any property system generates a range of possible interferences both legitimate and illegitimate, such a libertarian has no simple answers to the question: 'What property regime maximises liberty?'

The relationship between property and liberty does not, then, exhibit any simple correspondence between particular conceptions of liberty and particular property regimes (cf. Loevinsohn, 1977). Many aspects of property which may impinge on liberty are not problems concerned with individual or collective control of resources, and in any case societies need not be committed to an exclusively private or common property regime. Even if we take one form of property, like land or the means of production, we find arguments favouring or disfavouring private property within different conceptions of liberty and we find that disagreement about property arises from within the same broad conception of liberty because of dispute about the characteristics of institutions like the market.

A brief examination of a recent essay by G. A. Cohen will help to emphasise the difficulty of specifying a property regime which is most conducive to any particular conception of liberty. Cohen (1979, p.15) concludes: 'I have wanted to show that private property, and therefore capitalist society, limit liberty, but I have not said that they do so more than communal property and socialist society.' Cohen feels that all property rules limit liberty, and because all property rules are enmeshed in societies in which particular liberties are more or less enjoyed, we may not be able to decide whether socialist or capitalist society limits freedom the less. The view that all property rules limit freedom follows from the definition of liberty which Cohen uses in this particular essay. It is that 'when a man cannot do as he wishes, because others will interfere, he is unfree' (1979, p.11).

Cohen objects vehemently to a definition of unfreedom which discriminates between interferences, which talks about legitimate and illegitimate interferences, because such a definition 'misassimilates alien values to that of liberty' (1979, p.12). A definition which makes this distinction is termed by Cohen a moralised definition of liberty. The objection to moralised definitions is that they enable liberty to be exhibited as compatible with private property by a sleight of hand: private property makes certain interferences with other persons legitimate, and a man is wrongly supposed to be not unfree when he cannot do as he wishes because others will legitimately interfere. Such a definition of freedom imports the alien value of property into that of liberty, says Cohen, and must be rejected.

As Cohen (1979, p.14) explicitly recognises, the conclusion of this argument would apply to any system of property rules. The argument establishes that all systems of property limit freedom, and the objection to a moralised definition of liberty would hold whether the legitimacy of interference was given by a set of private property rules or by a set of common property rules. The definition of freedom on which it is based is interesting, but odd. To be fair, Cohen's argumentative strategy is to hoist an opponent with his own petard, to show that capitalism limits freedom, on his opponent's own definition of freedom, and despite his opponent's claims. The oddity of the definition consists in running together a negative libertarian concern with prevented action – being unable to do x – with a concern with the wishes of the agent. A consistent pure negative libertarian argues that a man is unfree if and only if he is prevented from doing x by other persons. Whether he wishes to do x is irrelevant, because as Berlin was quick to acknowledge, we do not want to generate a paradox by which a man can become more free by limiting his wishes (1969, p.xxxviii). In fact, despite Cohen's strictures, the definition is already 'moralised'. If I respect the property rules, and I therefore find it inconceivable even to wish to act in a way which is inconsistent with them, then the rules can never make me unfree.

Because property is concerned both with physical resources and with rules which define legitimate activity with respect to those resources, and because negative liberty may be construed in physical terms (the absence of prevention) and in rule-governed terms (the absence of legitimate interference) or in terms which embrace both (the absence of interference) it is important to be clear about the basis of any argument about the connection between negative liberty and property. We have seen first, that a pure negative libertarian can say little about the relationship between property rules and liberty, because those rules have only a contingent connection with the prevention of action. A moderate negative libertarian will find the problem complex, because the range of interference he is prepared to construe as reductions in freedom is wider, but property rules, like laws, distribute immunity to interference, and defining a set of such rules to produce a justifiable distribution of immunity from interference is challenging enough. If further problems arise because of the instability of the distribution of resources, it is even more difficult. If, however, a moralised definition of liberty is employed, legitimate interference (licensed by the property rules) is held not to restrict liberty: but then this is true whatever the rules are. In sum, for the pure negative libertarian conception, the contingency of the connection between property rules and prevented action hinders further analysis; for a conception which refuses to treat legitimate interference as a reduction of liberty no property rules impinge on liberty; and the moderate negative libertarian, who is concerned with a range of interferences, legitimate and otherwise, has an extremely complex problem. Hence just as a commitment to a positive conception of freedom, as we have seen, does not, without further assumptions, entail either support for state or common or private property, so a commitment to negative liberty does not lead inexorably to support for private property (cf. Gill, 1983, esp. p.694).

5 Property and Labour

There is a range of arguments about property which are enmeshed in different understandings of the necessity of labour and the extent to which it can be overcome. In this chapter we shall examine four of these arguments. The first advocates using the property system to provide individual workers with an incentive, and it was made explicit by James Mill (1978). The second is the theory that the labourer is entitled to a property in the product of his labour, a theory capable of many interpretations which is associated particularly with John Locke and Robert Nozick (e.g. Drury, 1982). The third is Hegel's idea that property is necessary to freedom, realised in acts of taking or making, and thus in labouring (e.g. Teichgraeber, 1977). The fourth is Marx's (e.g. 1977, pp.77–96) critique of alienated labour and private property under capitalism, his concern with the social character of labour, and the implications this has for 'co-operative' property. Our aim is not only to explain why the proponents of these theories were led to particular conclusions about desirable property arrangements by their various conceptions of the nature of labour and work, but also to scrutinise the conclusions drawn to see if they follow as readily as their advocates imagine.

Labour is necessary, in some form, if human life is to be possible. The Western tradition of political thought has been informed by a number of different understandings of the nature of this necessity, and of the extent to which particular persons, or man in general, can escape from it, overcome it or transcend it. While all four theories which we examine provide examples of such understandings, it will be helpful to discuss briefly two important sources of modern ideas: the classical Greek exclusion of most labourers from political participation and the Genesis story of the Fall. Both draw attention to a dualism which we shall notice in modern theories: on the one hand, labour is a painful necessity, imposed by man's needs and what he has to do to satisfy them; on the other, labour and work are a form of creative activity through which he can give himself expression and impose himself on his external world.

In *The Human Condition*, Hannah Arendt provided an interpretation of this dualism, in which she wrote eloquently of the Greek denial of the capacity of those engaged in labour to enjoy a full political life:

> 'Contempt for laboring, originally arising out of a passionate striving for freedom from necessity and a no less passionate impatience with every effort that left no trace, no monument, no great work worthy of remembrance, spread with the increasing demands of *polis* life upon the time of the citizens and its insistence on their abstention (*skholé*) from all but political activities, until it covered everything that demanded an effort. Earlier political custom, prior to the full development of the city-state, merely distinguished between slaves, vanquished enemies (*dmōes* or *douloi*), who were carried off to the victor's household with other loot where as household inmates (*oiketai* or *familiares*) they slaved for their own and their master's life, and the *dēmiourgoi*, the workmen of the people at large, who moved freely outside the private realm and within the public.'

She goes on to point out that later developments led to the classification of occupations according

> '. . . to the amount of effort required, so that Aristotle called those occupations the meanest "in which the body is most deteriorated". Although he refused to admit *banausoi* to citizenship, he would have accepted shepherds and painters (but neither peasants nor sculptors).' (1958, pp.81–2)

Slavery, of course, was the paradigm condition of persons locked into a sphere of necessity, whose purposes in life were exclusively the satisfaction of their own and others' needs. Other persons engaged in labour might also be more or less restricted in their purposes. The condition of the slave allowed the freedom of the master: the master could escape from the realm of necessity by domination of those whom he forced to provide for him, while his wealth gave him the opportunity to participate in common, public affairs. Under this understanding, *man* could not escape from necessary labour – or, rather, he could only if slaves were not treated as human. Freedom from necessity could be achieved by some at the expense of others, but could not be enjoyed by all. Those most clearly restricted by necessity, the slaves, were those without property, and those who could transcend it could do so only in virtue of their wealth.

There is another contrast to which Arendt's remarks draw attention: that between work devoted to the satisfaction of needs, which perishes when the need is satisfied, and the results of work which makes its mark on the world, and has some place in human history or public record. If some could escape from necessity by imposing labour on slaves, or by having the wealth to command the labour of workmen, others might possibly escape by devoting their efforts not to the satisfaction of needs but to the conscious shaping of the world. Human striving therefore had a dual character – it was imposed by need, but might be devoted to a more noble purpose and produce results which expressed something of those who had achieved them.

The story of the Fall unites an explanation of the necessity of burdensome labour with a notion that labour involves discharging a duty owed to God. Adam's expulsion from the Garden of Eden occurred when he had been told 'In the sweat of thy face shalt thou eat bread, till thou return unto the ground; for out of it wast thou taken; for dust thou *art*, and unto dust shalt thou return' (Genesis, 3.19). The necessity of burdensome labour may be seen as a punishment for Adam's transgression. He had, in his pre-lapsarian state, only to tend the garden, but now he is to exert himself to secure his living. Put another way, in the Garden of Eden, abundance is assured; but Adam's expulsion pitches men into a world where goods are scarce and must be won through labour. The story provides an explanation for the scarcity which secular thought also associates with the necessity of labour.

While labour could be seen as a punishment, it could also be regarded as a sign of gratitude to a God who had created man and his world, and given him the latter for his use. In labouring man obeys God's injunction to improve His gift, displaying his gratitude for the beneficence of his Creator. Hobbes (n.d., pp.235–6), for example, described labour both as a form of worship, through which man expressed his awe for his Creator while benefitting from

His gift, and as a necessary price to be paid for the enjoyment of resources. As we saw in Chapter 2, different accounts of the intention of the Creator have led to quite different accounts of the legitimacy of property. Particular property regimes have been seen by Christian writers as necessary to the character of fallen man, or necessary to encourage the discharge of his duties to God. If man is fallen, perhaps he is too selfish to be able to sustain common property; or perhaps private property reinforces or embodies the scarcity which is his punishment. Although the possession of private property might be sinful, fallen man is perhaps incapable of sustaining any other arrangement. The connection between labour and property in Christian theology, then, is informed by interpretations of the Creation, God's gift, and the story of the Fall.

For some writers, there was a closer connection between God's creative acts and the labour of man. God created the material of the world and formed it into the shape available to man. Man, too, could shape or transform his external world. There might therefore be an analogy between God's organising activity and man's transforming labour. Of course, there could be no analogy to God's creation of the world *ex nihilo*, the first act presupposed by any human activity, even if man could bring something 'new' into the world (Anselm, 1974, pp.18–20). One interpretation of the notion that God made man in his likeness was that he made man capable of creative activity. James Tully holds that a version of this analogy is a vital component in John Locke's theory of property (1980, pp.108–10). Locke attributed property to God because He was the Creator, and to man because he mixed his labour with God's gift. Locke's argument, detached from its theological premises, has been used by 'socialists' like Thomas Hodgskin (1832) and libertarians like Robert Nozick (1974) to determine the legitimacy of property.

The story of the Fall, then, provides a contrast between a world of plenty and a world of scarcity, and explains the necessity of burdensome labour in that world as a consequence of sin. But the Genesis story also invites reflection on the nature of creativity, and the extent to which man might emulate the Creator through his own activity. The dualism between labour as a curse, as activity necessarily devoted to satisfying need, and as an expression of some other – and higher – part of man's nature is again present.

The four approaches to property which flow from particular understandings of labour, which we now come to, treat this dualism with varying emphases. The 'incentive argument' concentrates on the necessity of labour for subsistence, while the labour entitlement theory, in Locke's hands, begins from the necessity of appropriation through labour to satisfy needs.

The labour entitlement theory, advanced by Locke, sets out from the necessity of appropriation by labour if needs are to be satisfied, but develops the argument as a justification of property in the results of a man's creative effort. Hegel does not deny that some labour appears to be merely instrumental, but he argues that an adequate understanding of the nature of property must grasp that property is an expression of personality, a consequence of man's shaping of his world. Marx's discussion of alienation rejects private property under capitalism because it reduces labour to need-satisfaction, while he advocates social property to allow for truly human, creative, production. These varying emphases, and the consequences drawn from them for property, are the subject of the rest of this chapter. We begin with the 'incentive argument', because it is straightforward and provides a convenient foundation for the contrasts to be drawn out.

Property as an incentive to labour

If labour is an unpleasant and painful activity – something made explicit in the curse of labour imposed on a rebellious Adam, but capable of secular formulation as a law of nature – then man requires a reward to overcome his disinclination to engage in it. Of course, threats, force and domination may make another person labour, but if there is to be personal freedom these procedures are excluded. If no one would labour without reward, then the property system should be consistent with the provision of this incentive. We may separate the claim that an individual deserves a reward for the expenditure of his labour, from the claim that a system in which the individual has an incentive is of general benefit. We have already encountered, in Chapter 2, the 'economic' argument that property rights should be structured to 'internalize externalities', to maximise both the benefits and costs of a person's activities which he bears. We have also met, in Chapter 4, the claim that private property is desirable because it is consistent with a market which promotes the general level of welfare. Both of these claims concern the benefits of the overall system, and may be separated from the argument that an individual labourer is entitled to something as a consequence of his activity, a claim which may be made without reference to the aggregate welfare.

The connection between 'incentives' and 'internalizing externalities' is clear enough. The incentive argument holds that a reward for labour is necessary to overcome the disutility of labouring. 'Internalizing externalities' aims both to maximise the amount of consequential benefit of labour which is enjoyed by the labourer, and to minimise the costs of his activity which are transferred to others. A group of individuals may collectively engage in hunting animals for food. It might occur to someone that a greater return for his own effort could be secured if he enclosed some animals and bred them. But this individual would receive a greater return for his own efforts (of enclosure and breeding) if he could exclude others from the benefits of his actions, rather than sharing with them, as he shares the spoils of the hunt. Since the hunting spoils *are* shared, additional effort by any one individual will not necessarily be fully rewarded. Exclusive enjoyment of the benefits of labour therefore increases the incentive to bestow it. So the connection between incentives and the economic argument that externalities should be internalised is made through the notion of exclusion.

All this is tied into the notion of a general benefit arising from such arrangements by invoking the importance of efficiency. If the level of welfare a society can achieve depends upon making the best use of resources, and if such use requires a particular set of property rights, which allow for internalising externalities, then the argument for providing an incentive to labour is not merely one of individual entitlement to a reward for labour. It is, rather, based on the welfare of all. The utilitarian efficiency argument may therefore be divorced from an argument for individual entitlement to a reward for labour in two ways. First, one could assert that entitlement on non-consequentialist grounds. Secondly, one could accept the social need to provide labour with an incentive without asserting that the individual *deserves* reward for any other reason.

It will be obvious that the notion that labour is unpleasant, and that individual reward is necessary to overcome a natural disinclination to labour, relies on a particular conception of human motivation. That view may be found in many writers, such as David

Hume and Adam Smith, but it is made most explicit by later utilitarians like Jeremy Bentham and James Mill. James Mill made the guarantee of property to the labourer a chief end of government. In his *Essay on Government*, he wrote that labour was imposed on man by scarcity.

'Of the laws of nature, on which the condition of man depends, that which is attended with the greatest number of consequences, is the necessity of labour for obtaining the means of subsistence, as well as the means of the greatest part of our pleasures.' (1978, p.56)

He went on to suggest that scarcity occasions conflict of interest, and thus the need for government. A high priority was given to arrangements concerning labour:

'When it is considered that most of the objects of desire, and even the means of subsistence, are the product of labour, it is evident that the means of insuring labour must be provided for as the foundation of all.' (1978, p.56)

The importance of 'incentives' was manifest:

'To obtain all the objects of desire in the greatest possible quantity, we must obtain labour in the greatest possible quantity; and, to obtain labour in the greatest possible quantity, we must raise to the greatest possible height the advantage attached to labour. It is impossible to attach to labour a greater degree of advantage than the whole of the product of labour . . . The greatest possible happiness of society is, therefore, attained by insuring to every man the greatest possible quantity of the produce of his labour.' (1978, p.57)

Mill was proposing this form of insurance as beneficial to all, as the best means of securing the greatest possible happiness of society. His prescription required the guarantee to each person of as much of the produce of his labour as possible. Not only does this view rely, as we have seen, on a particular theory of human motivation, or psychology, but also it relies on the assumption of a possible harmony of interest between individuals, secured through a market mechanism. That is, reward for labour is desirable for everyone in society because it produces the 'greatest possible happiness' through its effect on individuals. The idea is to provide individuals with the greatest possible incentive, which mobilises labour. The consequent production is socially advantageous. This reasoning is used, a century later, by the International Federation of Phonogram and Videogram Producers:

'The purpose of the copyright system has always been to promote cultural activity by granting the creators of musical or literary works exclusive rights to control the use of their intellectual property – thus providing them with the economic incentive to continue their creative endeavours for the benefit of all.' (1984, p.7)

Exclusive property rights create individual incentives and are for the general benefit.

One important aspect of 'insuring to every man the greatest possible quantity of his labour' is the need for security if incentives are to be as powerful as possible. Although incentives may be required to overcome the disutility of labour, the return for effort will be discounted in a rational calculation by the risk, if any, that the reward will not be obtained. There are many factors which contribute to such a risk, but two seem especially significant. The first is that the expected reward may not be received – for example, market conditions change adversely. The second is that although the reward is received, the individual cannot hold onto it in the face of encroachment from others – for example, he successfully harvests his crops only to find that others take his produce by violence.

The key notion is again excludability. To be secure in this enjoyment of an individualised incentive a person must be able to exclude others from the reward which he receives. Security was especially important to Jeremy Bentham and James Mill because they thought that frustrated expectations were a source of pain (or loss of happiness). And, of course, frustrated expectations may well result from insecurity. This negative evaluation of frustrated expectations had important consequences for their theory of property. They argued that no government – not even a representative one – should take away property which individuals had expected to enjoy (Lively and Rees, 1978, pp.43–4). This high valuation of the avoidance of frustrated expectations led to constraints upon justifiable redistributive policies. We saw in Chapter 4 that private property has been associated with negative liberty and restraint on government action in the history of liberal thought. The utilitarian argument of Bentham and Mill fills out the connections – private property is the reward for and incentive to labour, and it requires exclusion and therefore security, so government action must not frustrate expectations of the enjoyment of property.

There is only a contingent connection between the incentive argument and the utilitarian view of the undesirability of government interference with property. For Mill and Bentham, the connection was made through the high value of realized expectations. Some of the implications of this will be pursued in Chapter 6, where we shall discuss the problem of relating the longevity of property titles to the lives of individuals and to the time-span of resources. But we can see the contingency of the connection between the concern with incentives and the limitation on government action by glancing at the position advanced by Thomas Hobbes. Hobbes had also been keenly concerned with security in the affairs of men, and had taken the view that without security no-one would hazard his labour. His definition of property, like that of many seventeenth-century authors, was broad:

> 'Of things held in propriety, those that are dearest to a man are his own life and limbs; and in the next degree, in most men, those that concern conjugal affection; and after them, riches and the means of living.' (n.d., pp.223–4)

Hobbes's argument was that no-one living in a civil society could have property against the sovereign, because in the absence of the sovereign there could be no secure possession of any kind. The sovereign provided security, and this enabled a man to reap the benefit of his own activity: without the sovereign, 'property' would be too unstable to deserve the name. Hence Hobbes took a gloomy view of the prospects for property in a 'state of nature', in the absence of the overarching power of the sovereign:

> 'It is consequent also to the same condition, that there be no

propriety, no dominion, no *mine* and *thine* distinct; but only that
to be every man's, that he can get: and for so long, as he can keep
it.' (n.d., p.83)

'In such condition, there is no place for industry; because the fruit
thereof is uncertain: and consequently no culture of the earth . . .'
(n.d., p.82)

Before Bentham and Mill, Hobbes had held that security was
necessary before a man had an incentive to be industrious; but he
argued that this security was available only in a civil society
governed by a powerful sovereign, and that although such a society
allowed individuals property against each other, they could not
assert a claim to exclude the sovereign (e.g., n.d., p.133). The
utilitarians, by contrast, although they agreed that rights could be
guaranteed only by positive law, argued that security of property in
political society requires that the sovereign respect property. As we
saw in Chapter 4, a tension appeared when this argument was
combined with a commitment to an extensive franchise, for many
feared that the poor would use their power through the ballot box to
dispossess the rich and frustrate the expectations of the propertied.

There is a great deal of controversy about the proper relationship
between the expenditure of labour and the property system. This
controversy results partly from different conceptions of the
connections between labour and the product of labour, and partly
from conflicting assessments of 'labour'. We may illustrate some of
these issues by reference to the utilitarian argument we have
already examined.

First, the utilitarian argument we have reviewed is concerned
with incentives, and the possible harmony of interests in a market.
The guarantee to each of the greatest possible quantity of the
product of his labour is to secure the greatest happiness. As we have
seen, these consequentialist considerations should be distinguished
from claims that the individual labourer is entitled to a reward for
labour. This reward may be considered as a matter of desert, and
the labourer as deserving in the virtue of hard work or effort
expended, or (for reasons to be explained) because he has a right to
a property in what he produces. Although the 'incentive argument'
we have introduced is enmeshed in a utilitarian theory about the
possible harmony of interests, the 'desert argument' need not be. It

may simply be held that labour is deserving of reward, independently of the social benefit which might thereby result. The strongest version of the entitlement thesis argues for the individual's right to the product of his labour, which we shall examine in the next section.

A second controversy arises from different conceptions of labour because we do not necessarily have to characterize the labour which occurs in a social world as 'individual', in the way that the utilitarian argument does. There is often a problem of distinguishing individual contributions to a product, of delineating the elements attributable to the efforts of particular persons (Rawls, 1972, p.4; Nozick, 1974, pp.183–9). But apart from that pragmatic consideration, a more radical critique of the individualist conception arises from the theory that labour is, in some way, inherently social, and that the property system should be consistent with a recognition of the social character of labour.

A third dispute arising from alternative conceptions of labour may also be introduced by contrast with the utilitarian position. According to that view, labour is unpleasant, painful, and a source of disutility. But others have felt that labour need not be unpleasant. Two different versions of this claim may be distinguished initially. One holds that labour is liberating, that all work or labouring activity externalises the producer, puts him into the world, and is necessary to freedom. The second holds that although labour may well be a disutility under existing conditions (usually, and more specifically, capitalist conditions) it would not be if the property system were recast. In the next three sections, these alternative perspectives will be discussed – first, that an individual is entitled to the product of his labour, however conceived; secondly, that labour is liberating, an expression of personality; and thirdly, that labour is inherently social. Just as the utilitarian argument was used to support one conception of property, so each of these alternative perspectives has been thought to require particular property arrangements.

Individual entitlement to the product of labour

We saw in Chapter 2 that a crucial element in a complete account of 'property' or 'ownership' is an account of the means by which the title to property is acquired, transferred and lost. The notion that an individual is entitled to the product of his labour has been used as a theory of original just acquisition, a theory, that is, which aims to show how title to resources or 'things' could legitimately arise. Obviously, no account of the legitimacy of property transfers – by gift or by inheritance, for example – will answer the question of how property titles might legitimately have arisen in the first place. In this section we shall examine the theory that the expenditure of labour by individuals could ground such titles to property, and the difficulties which arise in attempting to apply the theory.

In Chapter 3 attention was drawn to John Locke's periodisation of property. According to him, 'private' property emerged from a condition of original communism, since the gift of the earth was made by God to all. In addition, we noticed in Chapter 4 that Locke's argument was based upon individual rights. It was suggested that although the overt form of the argument rested on the expenditure of labour, its premises (which were concerned with individual rights) could equally have been expressed in the language of liberty. Our first task, then, will be to explain the connection between the emergence of 'private' property, and the assertion of these rights.

Locke (1965, Chapter 5) interpreted the Genesis story to entail original communism: God's gift was to all, not to Adam as an individual. But although the world was given to all, each person had, according to Locke, a property in himself. This idea, of a property in oneself, sounds strange, but it is easily explicable. We do talk in at least possessive, if not proprietorial, terms when discussing control over our bodies. For example, one aspect of the contemporary debate about abortion concerns a woman's right to determine what she does with her body. Again, we may dispose of (parts of) our bodies, during our lives, by donating organs for transplant operations, and perhaps after our deaths, by committing them to medical research centres. Locke was concerned with a property in one's person, rather than one's body, and, as we shall see later, the idea of a 'person' is more complex than that of a 'body'. Two considerations will help to explain why Locke spoke in these terms. First, as Hobbes's remarks show, seventeenth-century authors gave property a wide meaning, and Locke was certainly not unique in thinking of 'self-propriety'. Secondly, Locke subjected the self-propriety of each to the duties he owed to God. Although the world was given to all, this did not apply to the individuals themselves. Each person was not a resource to be used by others, not common property, but his own man, himself. Pufendorf expressed this difference quite succinctly: resources given to all are in one way no-one's, but persons are not. Hence, he wrote, 'a man who belongs to no-one is not nobody's, but his own' (1710, p.320). Locke similarly held:

'Though the Earth, and all inferior Creatures be common to all Men, yet every Man has a *Property* in his own *Person*.' (1965, II, §27)

The notion of self-propriety is a restatement of the equal liberty of individuals in their original condition, where there is no natural political authority. No-one can legitimately claim power over another. 'Self-propriety', then, is designed to differentiate that part of God's creation which is common to all, from that part which is already particularised. The particularised created world provides a basis for the subsequent division of the common gift, a process of appropriation outlined in Chapter 3. So Locke's argument rests on liberty as well as the expenditure of labour and the notion of self-propriety both states the condition of equal liberty and the differentiation between the common and the particularised.

The passage from which the quotation above is taken links self-proprietorship with a property in labour:

'Though the Earth, and all inferior Creatures be common to all Men, yet every Man has a *Property* in his own *Person*. This no Body has any Right to but himself. The *Labour* of his Body, and the *Work* of his Hands, we may say, are properly his. Whatsoever then he removes out of the State that Nature hath provided, and left it in, he hath mixed his *Labour* with, and joyned to it something that is his own, and thereby makes it his *Property*.' (1965, II, §27)

Locke claims that since a person has a property in his own person, he has a property in his labour; and that if he mixes his labour with part of the common gift, it too becomes his. Property is attributed to the individual in virtue of the expenditure of his labour (generally, Menger, 1899). This argument has been popular amongst writers who have drawn very different conclusions from it, and most recently it has been revived by Robert Nozick in *Anarchy, State and Utopia*. We must now examine it more closely, and in particular explore the ambiguities surrounding what exactly the labourer is entitled to. These ambiguities help to explain why different conclusions for desirable property systems have been drawn from the same basic idea.

First, what is involved in the idea that a person has a property in his labour? We have already seen that the notion of self-propriety can be explained in terms of the individual's right to exclude others from interfering with his body and his liberty, to exclude others from control over the disposition of his person. To have a property in one's labour is to be similarly entitled to exclude others from control of that labour, to have the choices about its disposal in one's own hands. Both persons and labour, however, may come under the control of others. For example, slavery makes a property of another person, who loses his self-propriety because he has lost his freedom. Similarly, the activity of labouring may be directed by another person to whom the labourer has offered his services. A crucial distinction here is that between treating 'his' labour or 'his' person in an identifying or possessory way, and treating it in a proprietorial way (Day, 1966). For example, a slave is forced to work, but the labour he performs is still his labour, and 'his' body still identifies him as a distinct person. These are possessory uses. But the slave lacks the property in his person, since others own him, and he has no property in his labour, since it is not his to control, even if it is his in a possessory way. Hence, when Locke suggests that 'The Labour of his Body' is his, this is obviously true in the identifying sense of 'his', while the stronger proprietorial sense is treated as an implication of his property in his person. To claim a property in labour is to claim more than the trivial possession of a labouring capacity: it is to claim a right to determine how it is used, and hence to exclude others from its direction, control or, perhaps, result. For all of these – direction, control and result – are aspects of the use of labour. This ambiguity about 'his' is merely a particular reflection of the general difficulty we encountered in Chapter 2, namely that property refers to physical things and jural relations, just as in this context 'his' refers to a physical relation and to a jural one.

Locke appears to derive the property in one's labour from the property in one's person. Since a man has a property in his person, he has a property in his labour. But 'labour', and the 'work of his hands' are ambiguous (Day, 1966, p.220). This is because his 'work' may refer to (i) his task, (ii) his activity, and (iii) the result of his activity. 'Labour' may be substituted for 'work' in (i) and (ii). It will be seen that the assumed identity between his labour and the work of his hands imports, in addition to his control over his activity and the tasks he undertakes, control over the result of his activity. To have a property in his work as activity is, of course, not at all the same thing as having a property in the result of his labour. The first is analogous to his property in his labour, and may be treated as an implication of the freedom expressed by the notion of self-propriety. But the second is not analogous to his property in his labour, and thus needs further support – additional to that provided by 'self-proprietorship'. Even if his person and his labour are his own, why should he have a property in the result of his labour?

One answer which has been proposed as a key to the interpretation of Locke's version of the theory is that he subscribed to the workmanship model' (Tully, 1980, pp.35–6, 108–10), according to which there is an analogy between God's creation of the world and man's creation of his world in or through his activity. Just as Locke attributed a property in His creation to God, in virtue of His creative acts, so he attributed property to men in virtue of *their* creative acts, made evident in the results of their labour. In labouring, man is not only improving God's gift and obeying His injunction to be fruitful, but also he is reproducing some aspect of the original creative act. The validity of any such analogy between man and God is a matter of theological debate, but, in any case, the parallel between God's property in His creation and man's property in the result of his labour would leave the justification of both still to be explained.

This draws attention to an important aspect of the parallel and of the justification, namely that the notion of *exclusion* can be used negatively. That is, it may be argued that I have a right to the results of my labour, or, negatively, that no-one else has such a right, and therefore I have a pre-eminent claim. Locke is initially concerned, it will be recalled, with individual appropriation from the previously common gift. The analogy is supposed to be with God's creation of the world. Now in the second case, it is obviously plausible to suggest that God was prior, logically and temporally, to any other claimant to the world, and that He therefore has some exclusive claim. In the first case, individual labour may be interposed between the common gift and the commoners, because their claim is to the created world, whilst labour changes the form of that created world. They have no claim to the results of another man's labour, since the labour has added something additional to what was originally given (usefulness or value). Hence the labourer has a claim, but others do not, and, therefore, he is entitled to exclude them. This denial that others have a claim has a positive aspect: Locke's attempt to attach the results of labour to the activity of labour and thus to the person of the appropriator, to move resources from the category of common gift to that of the already particularised creation. But this denial also has a negative aspect: denying the claims of others. The acceptability of that denial depends on whether it is reasonable to suppose that they are at least as well provided for after the appropriation as before it. Since this suggestion forms part of the most modern use of the labour theory, in Nozick's account of original acquisition, we may leave it aside until we move on to that account.

Nevertheless, one of the implications of appropriation for others may be pursued here, because consideration of it will enable us to explore ambiguities in 'the result of his labour'. Locke's labour theory of just acquisition is concerned with the origin of private property in resources, or at least with the origin of exclusive use rights over them. It uses the application of labour to differentiate the common from 'the private'. The labour theory of property entitlement may also be applied at a second stage, when all the resources in the original gift have been particularised. Two important questions here are, first, to what exactly is the labourer entitled when he is no longer mixing his labour with *common* property? and, secondly, is there a clear connection between the theory of *original* just acquisition and an entitlement to the result of one's labour subsequently?

Let us suppose that all of the originally common property has become particularised. The application of labour to such particularised property clearly cannot have its original effect of distinguishing the 'private' from the 'common'. The labourer might, however, be conceived to have an entitlement to the result of his labour in some other or parallel sense. The possibilities here depend on two features of the organisation of 'production', namely on the organisation of markets, if any, and the extent of the division of labour. Three simple examples of 'production' will draw attention to the important variations. In the first case, which we may call the 'pure independent artisan model', there is no labour market. All producers work for themselves, and they do not hire the labour of others to assist them. In a particular trade, let us say that of the miller, goods which are to be worked upon are bought from another independent producer. For example, a farmer sells wheat to the miller, while the miller, who produces flour, sells it to the baker, who himself sells bread. Under these arrangements, each tradesman takes a resource which he alone works upon to produce a different marketed resource. In the second case, the 'integrated production model', let us suppose that the milling and baking enterprises have been combined. Again, there is no labour market; and each person works for himself. In the third case, 'integrated production with wage labour' the enterprise has expanded and labour is hired by the firm. The important variable features, then, are whether there is a labour market; whether each person is providing something identifiable as the product of his labour, and which products are marketed.

It will be clear that the possibilities of establishing a parallel between the labour theory of original just acquisition, and the labour theory of entitlement in a world of particularised resources, depend upon these three variable features. The parallels are closest in the 'pure independent artisan model'. The resources which are worked upon may be purchased, and become the property of the person performing the labour. His product is physically identifiable, and may itself be transferred in the market. The application of the notion of the labourer's entitlement looks fairly straightforward, because the product is wholly the product of one producer's labour and all the resources necessary to produce it are already his property before he applies his labour. The model, of course, assumes the legitimacy of the transfer of produced goods in virtue of that transfer recognizing the producer's entitlement. The parallel with the theory of original just acquisition is that in the pure independent artisan model one person's labour is embodied in a distinct physical product, and the model assumes that juristically everything brought to bear in the course of production belongs to the producer. In the model, this is because the producer can purchase his 'inputs'; in the theory of original just acquisition, it is because the producer has a property in his person and his labour.

In the 'integrated production model' matters are less simple. The miller and baker both work on the wheat which they jointly buy, and sell bread. Obviously the important difference between this and the previous model is the lack of a market for the 'intermediate good', flour. When producers co-operate without each producer putting his product into a market, and especially when there is no physically distinct product of an individual producer, the relationship between the final product and the labour of any particular producer is harder to establish: in joint production, what are the appropriate shares of the final product (if the product is physically divisible) or of its value?

The third model introduces the problem of a labour market, or of transferred labour. The 'firm' owns the productive resources and buys the wheat, but it employs others to convert it into bread. The problem in the 'integrated production model' is to determine the appropriate division of the return on the final product, when the producers themselves own the resources used in their joint production. In the third model, the producers do not own those resources, but those who do, the owners of the firm, are not themselves expending their labour in the process of making the bread which is to be sold. In the first two models, the entitlement of the labourer may be interpreted as an entitlement to (a share of) the physical product (or its value when sold). In the third model, individuals have sold their capacity to labour to the firm. The interpretation of the labourer's entitlement may then be (i) he continues to be entitled to the product of his labour, even if present arrangements wrongly deny it to him, (ii) the transfer of labour transfers the labourer's entitlement, so the person who purchases labour becomes entitled to the product of the labourer, especially when it is he, rather than the labourer, who owns the resources used in production, (iii) the labourer's entitlement changes its form, from an entitlement to the product of labour to a return for labour, from a juristic claim over the product to an entitlement to the value added by the expenditure of labour, or to the wages he receives when his labour is sold. The difference between (ii) and (iii) is that under (ii) the juristic claim is transferred, while under (iii) it is obliterated.

In the 'pure independent artisan model', and in the 'integrated production model', the labourer's entitlement may be treated as one to the physical product, or if he chooses to sell it, to the value of

his physical product. One interpretation of the labourer's
entitlement under the third model is that it continues to be to the
physical product. As we have seen, the problem here is that in the
third model the labourer owns neither the materials worked upon
nor the resources (other than his labour) used in his activity. Those
who have wanted to maintain the strong entitlement thesis have
therefore been driven to examine the legitimacy of the ownership of
the means of production by persons other than the direct producers
(Hodgskin, 1832), on the one hand, and to emphasise that all
resources are the product of labour, on the other, arguing that what
is produced should be the property of the associated producers,
rather than the property of those whose command over productive
resources enables them to hire the labour of others (Marx, e.g.,
1977, pp.114–22). This argument rapidly leads to challenging the
legitimacy of wage-labour associated with some forms of private
ownership of the means of production. The strong version of the
labour entitlement thesis, then, holds that wage-labour resting on
the private ownership of capital is incompatible with its recognition.

The second interpretation of the labourer's entitlement under the
wage-labour model supposes that the sale of labour involves a
transfer to the buyer of the labourer's entitlement. Locke himself
seems to have held this notion, for he argued that appropriation of
the common through labour extended to cases where one person
had control over the labour of another:

> 'Thus the Grass my Horse has bit; the Turfs my Servant has cut;
> and the Ore I have digg'd in any place where I have a right to them
> in common with others, become my *Property*, without the
> assignation or consent of any body.' (1965, II, §28)

There has been considerable dispute as to whether the relationship
Locke assumed between master and servant is properly conceived
as a wage-labour one, and it is clear that there are a number of
alternative grounds other than a wage-labour contract, on which the
master might be conceived to have a property in the results of his
servant's labour (Waldron, 1982; Tully, 1980, pp.135–42). But that
dispute is not critical to the present discussion, because it is
concerned with the alternative reasons for supposing that the
servant has transferred his labour. It is clear that Locke attributes a
property in the result of a servant's labour to his master. He is

suggesting that the master can claim an entitlement to the product of the servant's labour because the master rewards the servant for his activity, which is under the master's control. This interpretation separates the reward for labour as a juristic claim to the product of labour from the reward the labourer receives from employment, attributing the first to the master.

The third interpretation treats the labourer's entitlement, under conditions of wage-labour, as an entitlement to the value added by his labour or to the wages he receives. The value-added conception derives from a comparison of the third model with the other two already discussed. In the 'pure independent artisan' and in the 'integrated production' model, the producer's entitlement is primarily conceived as an entitlement to property in a physical product. But it may also be conceived as an entitlement to value-added, when the product is sold. Since the producers own the productive resources and the 'inputs', their property in their product and their entitlement to the value-added are the same. If the value-added is stressed, those two models and the third can be said to share a common feature: under the first two, the producer's entitlement is to the value he has added, and under a system of wage labour the same entitlement exists. The difference, of course, is that under the first two models the producers' property in the product is logically prior to the realisation of its value when it is sold, whilst in the third the payment the labourer receives is a contractual arrangement independent of the value received by the firm when the product, which is *its* property, is sold. Put another way, to have a property in the physical product is to have control over the disposition of resources, whilst to receive wages for producing a good which is the property of another does not have that consequence. The difference is a component of many objections to private property produced by wage-labour. Finally, we may note that value-added and wages received may or may not be equal, so the form in which this third interpretation is expressed is important.

Although we may appear to have moved a long way from the seventeenth-century theorising of John Locke, in this discussion of the labour-entitlement thesis, the appearance would be illusory. Locke himself had to deal with the relationship between the labour theory of original acquisition and the extent of the labourer's entitlement in a world of already particularised resources. The economic arrangements he assumed or 'justified' in his treatment of the issue are contested, some (e.g. Macpherson, 1962, pp.223–38) seeing him as an apologist for a capitalist market economy (a generalisation of our third model) and others (Tully, 1980, pp.144–5) holding rather that he envisaged a society of independent producers (our first model). Locke's theory has been used by liberal-socialists, like Thomas Hodgskin, to argue that, whatever conclusion Locke himself drew, the labourer's entitlement in a juridical sense, to a property in the product of his labour, could be recognized only if the first model replaced the third. In particular, Hodgskin (1832, pp.24–6) objected to the ownership of capital by those who had neither produced it nor expended their own labour in conjunction with it. On the other hand, Locke's theory, in a modified form, has been used to ground a modern anarcho-capitalist theory of original just acquisition, by Nozick (1974), and it is to this version of the theory that we now turn.

Nozick's concern is to argue against theories of distributive justice which appear to license state interference in the holdings of property, wealth or income which individuals have achieved. We have already seen, in Chapter 4, that a contrast can be drawn between the results of a process of market interactions, and the processes of the market. Nozick's (1975, p.163) major point is that patterned theories of distributive justice generate continuous interference to establish and maintain the favoured pattern. Any attempt to determine a 'fit' between a pattern of holdings and the pattern of need or desert (or whatever the theory favours) will artificially freeze a process in time. According to Nozick's view, we should, in our treatment of justice, be concerned with three aspects of holdings. These are a specification of how original acquisition could legitimately occur; a specification of how transfers of holdings could legitimately occur; and a principle of rectification which will tell us what to do if something illegitimate has in fact taken place in original acquisition or in transfer (1975, pp.150–3). Of these, the first aspect is crucial, since the others presuppose it.

This way of looking at justice obviously requires Nozick to discuss what the principle of original acquisition might be, and not surprisingly he looks to Locke to provide help. After noticing some of the difficulties we have already discussed, Nozick moves on to an aspect of Locke's theory which he calls the 'Lockean proviso'. We have mentioned that a labour theory of property entitlement partly depends upon denying to persons other than the labourer a claim on the product of his labour. We pointed out that the acceptability of this claim, in the theory advanced by Locke, depends on the argument that other persons are at least as well provided after the appropriation as before it. In other words, Locke asserts the positive argument that, in appropriating, a man mixes his labour with what was common, and thus makes it his own; and he supports this negatively by suggesting that there is no ground for objection from others if two conditions are met. These are first, that nothing wastes in the possession of the appropriator, and second, that 'enough and as good left in common for others' remains after the appropriation. Some doubt has been raised as to whether the two apparently separate constraints – of avoiding waste, and of leaving enough and as good – are both required (Waldron, 1979). But clearly, what is of interest is how the second is to be interpreted. What exactly does such a requirement, of leaving 'enough and as good in common', amount to?

Nozick distinguishes two variants of it, which he calls the stringent requirement and the weaker requirement. Having taken Locke's requirement to mean that the situation of others should not be worsened by an act of appropriation, he distinguishes two ways in which a person's situation could be 'worsened' – first, 'by losing the opportunity to improve his situation by a particular appropriation or any one', and secondly, 'by no longer being able to use freely (without appropriation) what he previously could' (1975, p.176). He then suggests that a 'stringent' limitation on appropriation would rule out the first and second of these methods of worsening the situation of others, while a 'weaker' limitation would rule out only the second. The stringent limitation focuses on a person's ability to appropriate resources, while the second focuses on his opportunity to use them. For Locke, of course, the need to use resources by consumption of them was part of his argument about the entitlement to appropriate. The crucial question is whether Locke's constraints should be interpreted as an attempt to guarantee that others should be able to satisfy their needs, or whether they imply that others should have the opportunity to appropriate. But in terms of the discussion earlier in this section, the difference in Nozick's formulations reflects the difference between the juridical claim to the product of one's labour and the claim to a return for labouring. There is a vast difference between expending labour so that one has a *property* in the product, and merely being able to *use* resources (which may well be someone else's). Nozick adopts the weaker limitation on original appropriation, to avoid the conclusion that the stringent limitation would not 'yield permanent and inheritable property rights' (1975, p.176). This decision seems to be based on his preference for those rights, for if he is correct, and if the proper limitation is the stringent one, then we should have to deny the legitimacy of many private property rights.

Even if the weak limitation is adopted, however, there is still the problem of applying it, of deciding in actual cases whether the 'Lockean proviso' has been violated. Some of the most acute problems of application arise from the passage of time: for, as Nozick is aware, the limit on appropriation will have consequences for the legitimacy of subsequent transfers of holdings. As he puts it, 'Each owner's title to his holding includes the historical shadow of the Lockean proviso on appropriation' (1975, p.180), for if the original appropriation were limited by the extent of opportunities left to others to use resources, then subsequent transfers must be too. We shall revert to problems of this kind in the next chapter.

A second problem which needs exploration is establishing the basis of comparison which is at issue when 'worsening' the situation of others is mentioned. Nozick notices the problem, but does little to pursue it. The limit on original appropriation requires that others should not be made worse off than they otherwise would be. Like Locke, Nozick seems to make this a matter of comparing two different economic systems: one in which no such appropriation is allowed, and one in which it is. The question then becomes: are individuals worse off in a private property regime than they would be if there were no original acquisition? Nozick's undeveloped answer is no: 'I believe that the free operation of a market system will not actually run afoul of the Lockean proviso' (1975, p.183). (We may, incidentally, remember the distinctions drawn in Chapter 4 between actual, ideal and possible markets at this point.) Locke similarly held, as we saw in Chapter 3, that a person at the bottom of the social hierarchy, the day-labourer, would be better-off in a monetised private property regime than in a system of unappropriated resources where there was no incentive to bestow labour. We might ask why the comparison should not be with another system of property entitlements or distribution. Nozick's answer to this is that individuals have rights, including the right to appropriate, and that our question raises the possibility of a violation of those rights which he wishes to prevent. Since he gives only cursory argument to support the attribution of those strong rights, further debate would have to focus on whether they can be justified (1975, pp.ix, 180–1).

Nevertheless, one point Nozick makes in this context is worthy of note. In supporting his theory of acquisition, Locke suggests that, far from worsening the situation of others, appropriation may improve it. Thus the appropriation of unused land benefits others by increasing the supply of food, if the appropriator farms it, while enclosing land reduces the territory over which an individual would need to hunt and forage, and thus releases land for others (to use or appropriate?) (1965, II, §§36–7). (Of course, other conditions would have to be met before this benefit was secured.) In Locke's case, these arguments appear to be additional support on utilitarian grounds for the entitlement theory which has its major premise in the notion of self-propriety. They can therefore be subjected to independent assessment. Nozick's argument allows for the suspension of an entitlement if the Lockean proviso is violated. For example, he suggests that:

'. . . a person may not appropriate the only water well in a desert and charge what he will. Nor may he charge what he will if he possesses one, and unfortunately it happens that all the water wells in the desert dry up, except for his. This unfortunate circumstance, admittedly no fault of his, brings into operation the Lockean proviso and limits his property rights.' (1975, p.180)

But, Nozick wants to insist, this is not because there is a utilitarian argument which specifies denying his property rights, but because his property rights are suspended by the very theory which grants them in the first place. By contrast, someone who invents a drug is entitled to charge others as much as he likes for it, for they have the same opportunity to invent it as he had (1975, p.181). So the constraints on original acquisition must not be treated as restrictions imposed by an overarching utilitarian argument, but as a method of recognising rights. As we saw in Chapter 3, theories which postulate natural rights face difficulties in reconciling the claims not only of persons in one generation, but also of individuals in subsequent generations. We shall pursue this problem with respect to several theories, including those of Locke and Nozick, in the next chapter.

In this section we have contrasted the labour entitlement theory, which attributes a property in the product of labour to the labourer, with the utilitarian argument sketched in the first section. We have seen that 'a property in the product of labour' is capable of many different interpretations. The rights-based thesis put forward by Locke and Nozick attempts to establish an entitlement to property deriving from acts of original acquisition. We have explored the difficulties of applying the labour theory of property entitlement, both to original acquisition and to circumstances in which resources are already attached to persons. In particular, we have stressed the distinction between a juristic claim to the product and a claim to a return for labour. We have also noticed that whereas Locke is willing to adduce utilitarian considerations to support his argument, Nozick disavows them. Finally, we may note that Locke's first argument for the necessity of appropriation is based on the satisfaction of needs, while his central idea that labour renders things useful emphasises the contribution which property makes to a comfortable life. Nozick concentrates on appropriation rather than the nature or purpose of labour, assuming that it proceeds by the expenditure of individual effort. In the next section we examine an argument which stresses the role of property in allowing for the expression of personality, and for the role of labour in moulding the world. In the fourth we look at the argument that production is necessarily social.

Property as fulfilment or objectification

The idea that private property is essential to the realisation of freedom, a freedom found in labour and work, was put forward by G. W. F. Hegel. His theory of property is concerned with the process by which an individual puts his personality into the world, and for this reason it has been seen by some writers as 'Lockean'. This interpretation treats Locke's notion of 'mixing labour' as resting on externalising personality, and it is misleading, as we shall see. Hegel's theory that labour or work could be a source of fulfilment has also been cited as a source for Marx's ideas about alienated and unalienated labour, which we shall come to in the next section, although, of course, Marx argued to a conclusion favouring social property while Hegel dismissed it as incompatible with 'the right of personality'.

Hegel's theory of property is embedded in a political theory and in a wider philosophy which certainly cannot be readily summarised (see Plant, 1984a). The most important point for present purposes is that Hegel's philosophical enterprise was to explain the world, to show how man could be 'at home' both within his political institutions and within the wider world of nature. He attempted to overcome the dualisms of the particular and the universal, or individual consciousness and what was external to it, in this explication – because, he thought, only by the resolution or transcendence of these dualisms, only by the appreciation that they were illusory, could man truly be 'at home'. An example of this thinking may be drawn directly from Hegel's discussion of property:

> 'As *immediate* individuality, a person in making decisions is related to a world of nature directly confronting him, and thus the personality of the will stands over against this world as something subjective. For personality, however, as inherently infinite and universal, the restriction of being only subjective is a contradiction and a nullity. Personality is that which struggles to lift itself above this restriction and to give itself reality, or in other words to claim that external world as its own.' (Knox, 1952, §39)

Although there are dangers in paraphrasing Hegel, this amounts to something like the following. An individual who takes decisions is in one sense related to the world outside him when his decisions take account of the way in which that world impinges upon him. But personality, what being a person involves, is not merely being impinged upon by something external to the person, which is a limited form of relation to the external world, but rather it includes 'giving itself reality', putting itself into that world. Since the latter relation between personality and the external world is more complete, achieving it overcomes the limitation of merely passive or reactive connection to that world.

'To claim that external world as its own' personality requires the institution of property. Property enables an individual to put his will into a 'thing'. (Hegel, incidentally, is conscious of the difficulty in deciding what counts as a 'thing' (Knox, 1952, §43), a difficulty we encountered in Chapter 2.) A person with a will is capable of achieving ends through the operation of his will, but 'things', with no ends or purposes of their own, obviously are not. Hence:

> 'A person has as his substantive end the right of putting his will into any and every thing and thereby making it his, because it has no such end in itself and derives its destiny and soul from his will. This is the absolute right of appropriation which man has over all "things".' (Knox, 1952, §44)

Hegel's notion of property is that property is a realisation of freedom. While Locke's argument about individual entitlement to appropriate treats labour as necessary to the satisfaction of needs, and uses the satisfaction of needs as one justification for appropriation through labour, Hegel suggests that this is an inadequate conception of the relation between 'person' and 'thing' involved.

> 'If emphasis is placed on my needs, then the possession of property appears as a means to their satisfaction, but the true position is that, from the standpoint of freedom, property is the first embodiment of freedom and so is in itself a substantive end.' (Knox, 1952, §45)

Property, then, is not merely instrumentally desirable as facilitating the satisfaction of needs; it is an end in itself, because it provides freedom. This 'freedom' consists in overcoming the limitation mentioned earlier – freedom requires at a minimum giving personality a reality in the world outside the person. An immediate implication of this is that property is necessarily private, because any common property arrangement 'violates the right of personality' (Knox, 1952, §46). Private property may certainly be subordinated to the requirements of a rational state, but the rational state is a higher form of expression of personality and no violation is thereby occasioned.

Whilst there is some development of personality – some freedom – in the relation between an individual will and a 'thing', another vital aspect is the relation between the property-taker and other persons. Property which is 'taken' enables *others* to recognise the will, and hence the personality, of the taker. Since occupancy of the 'thing' is essential to this recognition, Hegel spends some time discussing exactly what it involves (Knox, 1952, §§54–58). The three forms of taking possession of a thing which he distinguishes correspond to different relations between the will and the thing. Hence physical possession is the most direct form of this relation – when I grasp something, my will is 'in' it quite clearly. Secondly, in forming something I put my will 'in' it, but my personality continues to be present in the shaped object, even if I am not directly associated with it by grasping it at present. Thirdly, my will may in some loose sense be 'in' something I mark as my own.

Although the simplest relation between a person and thing exists in these various ways of taking possession, the use of an object employs more complex connections. Hegel is critical of any distinction between ownership and use, because he thinks that full or complete use *is* ownership:

> 'Over and above the entirety of its use, there is nothing left of the thing which could be the property of another.' (Knox, 1952, §61)

Although he recognises that some property systems, like feudalism, detach title from use, he regards this as a limitation on freedom, since it prevents the full realisation of personality in the used object. So he argues:

> 'It is about a millenium and a half since the freedom of personality began through the spread of Christianity to blossom and gain recognition as a universal principle from a part, though still a small part, of the human race. But it was only yesterday, we might say, that the principle of freedom of property became recognised in some places.' (Knox, 1952, §62)

Adam Smith, we may recall, bemoaned feudal hangovers in a commercial society as an encumbrance to individualism and to the system of liberty which a commercial society made possible (above, p.59). Hegel similarly regrets the lingering vestiges of the feudal property system as an impediment to freedom, but 'freedom' here is the realisation of personality rather than individual political and economic liberty.

Even in alienating property I exhibit a relation between it and my will, since I withdraw my will from it and put it away from me. I may alienate the products of my skills or the use of my abilities or power to act for a limited period. This limitation follows from Hegel's notion that full use exhausts ownership. To give another person the *full* use of my powers would annihilate my will (Knox, 1952, §67). Because I can alienate something, I can engage in reciprocal arrangements or contracts which produce a limited participation in a will which unites me with another person: I participate, in respect of that contract, in a common will (Knox, 1952, §74). The end of the development with which Hegel is dealing is my participation in a general will of citizens realised in a rational state, and contract is by contrast a very limited form of participation in a communal will.

We have seen that moulding an object is one of the ways in which a person can take possession of a thing. It is a more developed form of possession than merely grasping a thing, because the will and consciousness of the person who, for example, makes a statue (to use Hegel's example (Knox, 1952, §68)) remains when the sculptor is not present, and even when he is dead. This shaping of nature is a form of work, but man naturally has to 'work' to make the world useful:

> 'There is hardly any raw material which does not need to be worked on before use. Even air has to be worked for because we have to warm it. It is by the sweat of his brow and the toil of his hands that man obtains the means to satisfy his needs.' (Knox, 1952, §196A)

Hegel is obviously alluding to the curse of Adam here, but because, as we have seen, he regards property as an embodiment of freedom, and because taking possession requires an act of appropriation or externalisation of will, Hegel does not have a wholly negative conception of labour imposed on man by natural necessity. Rather there is a 'moment of liberation intrinsic to work' (Knox, 1952, §194), because through work man shapes the world to his will, a world which would otherwise be merely an external source of impingement. As Plant has written:

> 'Labour is the way *par excellence* through which man moulds the world to his own patterns of meaning, transforming it to satisfy his own desires and is able to see in such transformations the reflection of his own personality.' (1984a, p.108)

We have separated Hegel's argument from the others in this chapter to illustrate the claim that different conceptions of the nature of labour lead to varying conclusions about desirable property arrangements. We should notice, however, that Hegel is not concerned with the *justification* of property as such; rather, he is concerned to *explain* it, to make the institution of property understandable within a broad pattern presupposing an abstract individual confronted by an external world who finds his home as a citizen of a rational state. Within this 'development' an important tension appears, one of which Hegel was acutely aware, and one which T. H. Green's worries about the rationale of property reflect. Property is, for Hegel, an externalisation of personality, making possible, through contract, participation in a common will. What, then, is the position of propertyless persons? Hegel was aware of the tendency to inequality in market systems. Those who have no property do not objectify their wills, and are unfree. It is not obvious that redistributive policies of the state or acts of private charity, even if they secure a propertyless individual against need, will overcome the lack of opportunity for objectification. Again, Hegel saw the state as a self-conscious form of association which would transcend the accidental and contingent association of each with all found in civil society, based on property, the division of labour and commercial interaction. The regulation of property and contract is primarily a matter for civil society, but if the consequences of the operation of economic forces within civil society are pauperism, the state may feel called upon to intervene. This intervention, however, undermines the distinction between state and society. Put another way: the form of association at the level of the state requires a contrast with a separate sphere in which individuals pursue their private purposes. The state may legitimately regulate property, but in doing so it undermines the contrast between the two spheres and begins to partake of private interests.

The tension here – property embodies personality and makes possible the arrangements of civil society, which may themselves produce impoverishment and propertylessness – is the source of Green's worry. His remark that propertylessness may undermine the rationale for property, which for him was the possibility of living a moral life as an expression of will, might also be applied to the theory advanced by Hegel. If property enables individuals to objectify their wills, to enter contractual arrangements and to participate in a common will, it may also be implicated in producing the inequalities which deprive some persons of these possibilities. It is a matter of some dispute as to how Hegel himself reacted to this tension, but he was certainly aware of it (Plant, 1980; Ritter, 1968; Stillman, 1980; Teichgraeber, 1977; Avineri, 1972, pp.150–4; Plant, 1984a).

The outline of Hegel's theory of property put forward here is taken from the *Philosophy of Right*, but that is not the only source for a full account of his ideas. It has been used because it is a late work and because the theory of property advanced in it is part of a wider political theory addressed to providing an explanation of the nature of the state. It is also the most accessible work in which some have found the 'Lockean' concept of property, a claim which we shall assess briefly below. We must first note that although Hegel explained the necessity of private property by reference to freedom, he also regarded private property as a contradiction, from the point of view of an individual, until its full social significance was grasped. Property is self-contradictory because it is to be used, and used up; but property establishes a permanent connection between a person and a thing. It is also self-contradictory because it allows others to recognise the personality of its owner, but in a respect in which he is equal to others, as an owner, not as a particular person. Thirdly, property is self-contradictory because it belongs to one person, but it has an existence for everyone. The freedom of externalisation and the recognition accorded to persons through property require participation in a fuller social existence to give them meaning (1949, pp.447–9). Hegel therefore saw private property as a necessary but inadequate aspect of overcoming the apparent dualism between individual consciousness and the external world.

Couched in less abstract language, Hegel's conception of property as an expression of personality, and his notion that other persons recognise an individual through the externalised sphere he creates through his property, has some appeal. It seems to explain, for example, some of the psychological attachment individuals feel towards their private realm, and thus the feeling of violation experienced when someone discovers that his home has been ransacked (Trasler, 1982). In liberal thought, this private sphere associated with private property has been valued as an arena in which the individual is secure from the actions of the state and which offers a buffer between himself and others. In particular, the

Lockean idea of life, liberty and estate envisages property as 'moral space', within which an individual has control over his own affairs. Again, Grotius (1853, vol. 1. pp.5–6) adopted the idea that justice consisted in giving each his due: constituting his 'due' by a set of rights, including property rights, which allocated a particular individual his share of this moral space. Locke's theory is predicated on natural rights, and he has to show that this sphere may be made available to all. Hegel is not concerned with natural rights as such, but he has to show that recognition of the 'right of personality' for some will not prevent the same recognition being accorded to others.

It is this connection between the externalisation of will in Hegel's theory of property, and mixing labour with the common gift in Locke's theory, which has led some writers to regard Hegel's account as 'Lockean' (Cullen, 1979, p.16). It is true that Locke begins with a property in one's person, and its subsequent mixing with the external world of the common gift, and that Hegel begins with personality and its 'subsequent' externalisation. The interpretation of Locke which stresses the importance of the 'workmanship model' also draws the two theories together. But there remains a fundamental difference. Locke's account begins from the necessity of appropriation if needs are to be satisfied, and this necessity is one of his strongest arguments against the consent theory of division of the common gift. Hegel's theory begins from a conception of externalisation based upon the development of freedom. Once the Lockean private sphere exists, it may well create a private realm within which freedom may be exercised, and of course Locke limited the legitimacy of interference with that property by the political association. Although the interpretation of Locke which emphasises the 'workmanship model' narrows the gap between the two approaches, the fundamental difference is that between Locke's instrumental argument for the necessity of appropriation to keep body and soul together, and Hegel's expressivist argument for property which allows the will to escape from subjectivity (cf. Ryan, 1984, Chapters 1 and 5).

Private property and alienated labour

We saw earlier in this chapter that the theory of the labourer's entitlement to a property in the product of his labour becomes difficult to interpret in an economy in which there is a labour market. In particular, we noted that if the producer is in a labour market but not a product market then he will not usually have control over the disposition of his product, although such control seems to be the core idea in the labour entitlement theory. This 'lack of control' is a central feature in Marx's treatment of alienation. He identified wage-labour and capitalist private-property as causes of that condition. Although he thought that Smith's analysis of the labour origin of property – discussed in Chapter 3 – was a step forward, he nevertheless held that political economy in general had failed to see the true connection between private property and labour because it took for granted capitalist private property without seeing it as alienated labour (1977, p.56). In this section we shall examine the notion of alienation and the accompanying theories of what constitutes human production, because this understanding of the nature of labour has quite different implications to the theories we have so far examined.

The most famous exposition of Marx's view of alienated labour is to be found in his *Economic and Philosopical Manuscripts*. Marx set himself a large task:

> 'So what we have to understand now is the essential connection of private property, selfishness, the separation of labour, capital, and landed property, of the value and degradation of man, of monopoly and competition, etc. – the connection of all this alienation with the money system.' (1977, p.78)

'All this alienation' clearly covers a great deal: private property; a particular disposition of character, namely selfishness; the consequences of separating labour from productive resources; the economic and social relations involved in competition and monopoly; and the degradation of man. Looked at in this way, private property is only a part of the problem of alienation, but because of the interconnectedness of the various aspects it is in many ways a focus of these concerns.

'Alienation', for Marx, involves the denial of something essential to man's nature, and the various forms of it are varieties of this central meaning. It follows from this, of course, that whilst the discussion of alienation picks out undesirable features of arrangements under capitalism, it also contributes to a picture of the circumstances which would be consonant with man's true nature (Geras, 1983); a world without alienation. Insofar as private property is implicated in the causes of alienation, then, some implicit account of arrangements which would avoid alienation should be derivable. Our discussion of alienation will therefore concentrate on these implications for property, as well as the criticism of capitalist property systems.

Marx (1977, pp.78–80) first of all points to the alienation of the producer from the object of his labour. The object is alienated, it confronts the labourer as an alien thing. All production is a realisation or objectification of labour, so the object on which a man works objectifies him. It is an external embodiment of his nature. Production is thus an expressive activity, and it should be pleasurable, because it makes this objectification possible. But before a man can express himself in his object, it must be under his control. For a wage-labourer under capitalism, however, this condition is not met. No sooner does he finish his product than it is taken from him. Labour should be a reflective and creative activity, but if a man's production is not under his control, then what he makes is not a product of his creativity, and once again his object is alien to him. Whilst, under proper conditions, the more a man produces the more he puts himself in the world and is fulfilled, under capitalist conditions the more he produces the more the world of objects is alien to him. Instead of work being life itself, instead of productive activity constituting life, it becomes merely a means to physical subsistence. This is because it is only the object of labour which enables a man to receive the means of subsistence and the means of work – objects must be produced in order to gain access to more work.

The second form of this alienation is from the activity of labouring (1977, pp.80–1). This externality of working arises because work is not an expression of creativity and is not a result of my free activity undertaken at my own volition. Furthermore, labouring does not satisfy a need, but merely enables needs to be satisfied. Indeed, a man's labour itself becomes someone else's when he sells his capacities to a capitalist. The particular inversion which Marx suggests to summarise all this is that man becomes animal in his human functions, and human in his animal functions. In those respects in which he should be asserting his humanity, through his creative activity, he operates merely as animals do, satisfying needs, while he feels himself only in those respects in which he is like an animal. This brings us to the crucial notion of human production, and its distinction from animal production, for Marx's notion of human production is the basis both for his criticism of alienated labour under capitalism and of his proposals for an alternative economic (and, therefore, property) regime.

According to Marx (1977, pp.81–3), man relates himself to the species of which he is a part. He uses a greater part of nature for his subsistence and his vital activity than other species, for the whole of nature is his: he works on it, transforms it, and is provided for out of it. Other animals, however, use only that part of nature which is specific to their species. Here we are given more clues as to what allegedly distinguishes human from animal production. Animals produce only under the impulse of need, whereas man produces in the true sense only when he is free from need. This illuminates further the earlier complaint that alienated labour is performed merely as a means to survival. In addition:

> 'Labour is in the first place a process in which both man and Nature participate, and in which man of his own accord starts, regulates and controls the material re-actions between himself and Nature. . . . By thus acting on the external world and changing it, he at the same time changes his own nature. . . . We are not now dealing with those primitive instinctive forms of labour that remind us of the mere animal. . . . We pre-suppose labour in a form that stamps it as exclusively human. A spider conducts operations that resemble those of a weaver, and a bee puts to shame many an architect in the construction of her cells. But what distinguishes the worst architect from the best of bees is this, that the architect raises his structure in imagination before he erects it in reality.' (1974, pp.173–4)

The elaboration of these remarks identifies these differences: man has a conception of what he wants to produce before he starts work, but (other) animals do not; man changes his own nature in his dealings with the external world, but animals do not; the needs of animals are fixed and constant, but man multiplies his; animals produce only themselves, but man produces all nature; man can separate his product from himself, whereas animals cannot; man has an aesthetic sense, but animals do not, even if man finds their products beautiful. Finally, man truly produces only beyond necessity, whereas animals produce because of it. But alienated man does not relate to his species as he might. His species-life, what is distinctly human, becomes merely a means to an end he shares with animals, namely survival.

Finally, while alienated labour separates a man from his species-life, from his true humanity, it also separates man from man (1977, p.83). Since each is alienated from his species-life, all are alienated from each other. Both capitalist and proletarian are alienated: the first, in what he does not do, and the second in what he does. Neither is involved in truly human production. The capitalist owns the object, but he did not produce it. He directed the labour involved, but it was not his own activity. The capitalist, just like the worker, is dependent on economic forces outside his control. Nor does the capitalist care what happens to the product once it is sold.

Wage-labour and private property are both implicated in the diagnosis of alienation. Private property under capitalism is the product of alienated labour, and wages are paid to workers who are alienated. It would appear, therefore, that both private property and wage-labour must be abolished if alienation is to be dispelled. In conditions of alienation, the relations between men appear as relations between things rather than as directly human relations. This is what Marx meant by the fetishism of commodities; 'the relation of the producers to the sum total of their labour is presented to them as a social relation, existing not between themselves, but between the products of their labour' (1974, p.77). These products are, of course, commodities, and the exchange of commodities, each of which is objectified labour, disguises from men the social character of their production. It *is* social, because the use-value produced by one man's labour is useful in relation to a human need, but the exchange transaction makes the producer indifferent to the need finally satisfied and concerned only with the market transaction. Similarly, the person who finally uses a product does not care about, and may have no knowledge of, the person who produced it.

The major critical point which Marx makes against capitalist private property, then, is that private property is the result of alienated labour. His conception of human production as species-activity, of the social character of labour, demands, he thinks, the abolition of that form of private property. As we saw earlier, the negative picture of alienation discloses also an image of an unalienated world, and Marx obviously held that social property was alone consistent with recognition of the social character of labour. The question of whether alienation, as described in the *Economic and Philosophical Manuscripts*, *could* be overcome under a system of social property is not, however, a straightforward one. For example, Marx is there concerned with the worker's ability to realise himself in his work, and the consequent need to control his production and the object of it. But we saw in Chapter 4 that equal control of productive activity may not be achievable for everyone except through social control of productive activity, which may allow each worker equal control over the production of all, but does not allow each exclusive control over his own activity. Indeed, maximising control over one's own production and its objects might well require the sort of society based on independent producers (based on private property, but with no wage-labour) which we encountered earlier. Of course, this would not overcome the other aspect of alienation which Marx identified, namely the effect which commodity production has on disguising from producers their true species character. Full control over the object of labour suggests the need for exclusive property, but this would require a market for products which would alienate each from his social species-life. But *social* control over production might equally prevent any one individual realising himself in his activity.

These points seem to be partially recognised in Marx's *Excerpt Notes on James Mill* (1977, pp.114–22). There he argues that the exchange relationship – based, of course, on private property – is the major barrier to man's realisation of the social character of labour. He proposes instead the direct satisfaction of another's need, apparently suggesting that alienation could be overcome if one man's production were directly for the use of another, and the relationship between the two were not mediated by market transactions. Under such circumstances, Marx suggests, 'My work would be a free expression of my life, and therefore a free enjoyment of my life' (1977, p.122). Although this is said to require the abolition of capitalist private property and of wage-labour, it again seems consistent with autonomously-directed but not self-sufficient production, although for the direct satisfaction of a human need rather than for the market. For these reasons, then, the negative implications of Marx's theory of alienation for a desirable property regime certainly include abolition of wage-labour and capitalist private property, but we may not share Marx's confidence that social property would overcome the alienation which he diagnosed.

Clearly, Marx's understanding of the proper relationship between labour and property is quite different from that adopted by the theorists already discussed in this chapter. Unlike the utilitarians, he denies that labour is merely a painful necessity to be overcome by rewarding individual workers, although he claims that under capitalism labour is reduced to a necessary means of survival. Unlike the labour entitlement theorists, he does not regard private property as an entitlement secured by the expenditure of labour, although he does condemn the alienation caused by the worker's loss of control over his object. James Mill wished to guarantee to a man 'the greatest possible quantity of the product of his labour', the entitlement theory accords property in the result of labour (variously conceived), Hegel's theory requires that property be private, or individual – but Marx holds that property should reflect the social character of production itself. Finally, as Becker (1977, p.121) has pointed out, '. . . the root idea of the labor theory seems inconsistent with the communism which is to result from the classless society in which labor has become unalienated' – if, indeed, communism will overcome alienation.

Marx's concern is not to secure to the worker the full fruits of his labour, but rather to secure to the associated labourers control over their joint production. He insisted that it would be a mistake to divorce distribution from production:

'If the material conditions of production are the co-operative property of the workers themselves, then there likewise results a distribution of the means of consumption different from the present one. Vulgar socialism (and from it in turn a section of the democracy) has taken over from the bourgeois economists the consideration and treatment of distribution as independent of the mode of production and hence the presentation of socialism as turning principally on distribution.' (1977, p.570)

Whatever system of property is advocated, we may add, we shall want to know the arrangements governing production and distribution which are thought to be consonant with it, and we shall want to subject these claims of consonance to critical scrutiny. We may be sceptical that 'co-operative property' will overcome all forms of alienation, just as we may be sceptical about the capacity of markets to avoid violation of the 'Lockean proviso'.

This chapter has contrasted four approaches to property which are associated with particular understandings of the nature of labour. The sharp separation between these approaches which has been employed to illustrate some of the issues surrounding the political theory of property should not, of course, be taken to suggest that no author draws on more than one of them. Locke introduced claims about the general level of welfare in society to bolster his theory of individual entitlement, and Hegel recognised that labour was often a matter of sweat and toil even if it was necessary to realise some freedom. The theories which we have encountered draw on both parts of the dualism between labour treated as a painful necessity and as expressive and creative activity. The incentive argument sees labour as a disutility, which Hegel acknowledged but regarded as an incomplete understanding in relation to property. Marx analysed alienation which arose from wage-labour under a capitalist private property system, and was confident that it could be overcome, or at least substantially reduced, under a system of social property. The labour theory of property entitlement focuses on appropriation as a form of labour, but while Locke's conception of labour stresses its contribution to making nature useful, Nozick draws on the notions of invention and creativity in defence of the idea that 'appropriation' need not worsen the situation of others.

We have also seen that the conception of labour adopted by a theorist does not itself generate a prescription for a property system. For example, a belief that the labourer is entitled to a property in the product of his labour may be shared by thinkers who disagree about its interpretation or about the economic arrangements which are consistent with its recognition. Again, commitment to the utilitarian concern to maximise the 'greatest happiness of the greatest number' does not entail commitment to James Mill's analysis of the best method to achieve it. Finally, a concern to provide workers with control over their products may be shared by theorists with different understandings of how it might best be provided. This conclusion is scarcely surprising, since we have already seen that adopting a particular conception of liberty does not lead to a desirable property system until many other assumptions are introduced.

6 Property and Time

A simple fact which is already familiar is that the time-spans of persons, resources and legal titles do not necessarily coincide. The consequences of this fact, however, are not at all simple. Examples of the questions which arise are should inheritance be allowed, or more generally what should happen to individual property on the death of its present holder? Secondly, since resources may be 'used up' to a greater or lesser extent by those to whom they are available, should these persons be entitled to use them as they please, or do they have obligations towards their successors which would limit their own actions? Thirdly, since property has been passed on from predecessors, do the present holders have any obligations towards those who went before, or obligations to their contemporaries which follow from the provenance of what they possess (such as providing access to works of art, or preserving the heritage of a nation)?

Although title outlasts particular individuals in modern private-property systems, so that ownership is transmitted to heirs, title is not always attached to natural persons. For example, if property is given in trust for some purpose, the title will be vested in a group of trustees, to deal with as the donor directed. The trustees may be individuals or institutions, like a bank. Even if one trustee dies, others will remain, and the total number necessary can be made up by addition when required. Institutional property, such as that of a business firm, is only indirectly attached to individuals, for example through the system of shareholding. Again, the state does not die in quite the same sense as persons. Property rules dealing with artificial persons like corporations will need to specify what is to happen to property in the event of something analogous to death – like bankruptcy or insolvency – befalling the business.

Inheritance

The simplest case from which to begin is that of inheritance within the liberal model described by Honoré and discussed in Chapter 2. Although transmissibility may be recognised by all *mature* legal systems, the terms on which transmission has been allowed, if at all, have been very variable (Simpson, 1965). In particular, the degree to which a present owner should be allowed to 'reach into the future' in the settlement of his property has been contested normatively and within legal practice. And sometimes the central concern has been the right to inherit property, rather than the right to bequeath it. The importance of this distinction needs elaboration. That the owner's will is to be respected in the disposition of his property after his death is part of the contemporary conception of inheritance. Legal provision for what is to happen in the absence of a will is modelled on a presumption about what the owner would have included in a will, had he made one. But the extent to which the owner's will is to be allowed to determine how his property should be distributed after his death has varied enormously. We may construct a spectrum representing different answers to the question, 'to what extent should the distribution of property after a person's death depend on that person's will?' At one end, the disposition of a person's property would be wholly under his control: his will would be operative in every detail. At the other extreme, his property would be subject to the operation of legal rules under which his wishes count for nothing. There are many intermediate positions – for example, a person may dispose of his personal property by testament, but the heir of his real property is determined by the law, not his will; or a fixed proportion of his property must be left to his family, while he is allowed to dispose of the rest as he wishes; or his will is in general respected, but he is not allowed to place conditions on the enjoyment of his property. Obviously, any position on this spectrum which is not the extreme one of respecting the owner's wishes in every detail will represent a compromise between the consideration due to the wishes of the present owner and other concerns, such as a desire to stabilise the pattern of landholding or to attend to the welfare of the testator's family.

Inheritance is, of course, only one answer to the question of how to treat property when the present owner dies. Another response would exclude transmissibility, for example by treating a dead person's property as *res nullius* and specifying how others might acquire a title to it, perhaps by occupancy. Again, the property rules might exclude inheritance by requiring a dead person's estate to pass to the state, possibly coupled with further specifications about what the state is to do with it. Because of the variations within the practice of inheritance, and because inheritance is not the only solution to the treatment of property at the death of its holder, it is a practice which needs justification.

Two preliminary points about justification may be made. First, inheritance involves a donor and a recipient, and some attempts to justify inheritance are attempts to legitimise the right of bequest, the power of the present owner to dispose of his property through a will. But others are attempts to justify the right to receive the property. It should be obvious that a right to receive the property may well be incompatible with a right of bequest (since the owner may not choose to leave the property to the person who has a 'right' to receive it.) Hence a justification of a right to receive a dead person's property is certainly a justification of inheritance, but it is not a justification for the right of bequest.

The second point is the close connection between alienability and hereditability. If a person sells his goods, he transfers them between living persons. If he disposes of them by will, he transmits them at death. In both cases there is some relation between the will of the propertied person and the disposal of his property. The recipient gets a good title whether the transfer to him be by gift, sale or bequest. Because both alienability and hereditability have an impact on the distribution of property, they are often considered together in discussions of property. The connection between them is also conceptual. If a person has transferred all his property *inter vivos*, he leaves nothing to inherit. Again, an extended power of bequest would limit the extent to which successors could alienate the property. Thirdly, if there is a strong right to inherit property, then the present owner may not be entitled to dispose of it in his lifetime. Fourthly, if death duties are avoidable by *inter vivos* transfer, such transfers may need to be regulated as well. These are four examples of the reciprocal connections between alienability and hereditability which draw attention to the implications of the extent of one for the other.

Having already distinguished attempts to justify the power of bequest from attempts to justify the right to inherit, we may begin our examination of inheritance practices with John Locke's argument for the right to inherit (cf. Waldron, 1981). This is not, to repeat, an argument for the standing of the will of the person bequeathing property. It is a claim that particular persons are entitled to receive the property of the deceased person. Locke talked of appropriation into the family unit, even though his initial examples are of direct appropriation to satisfy individual need, by taking and eating food (1965, I, §88). Since appropriation added to the family stock, the death of one member of the family reduced both the number of claims over the joint possessions and the amount of labour which could be expended in acquiring them. While the children's right to preservation gave them a claim over the family property while the parent lived, it also sustained a right to inherit when the parent died (1965, II §89). Locke left several aspects of the natural right to inherit unclear. In particular, it is not easy to tell whether he thought the child was entitled to a sufficient share to avoid the danger of extinction, or to whatever goods his parent left behind (II §183, II §65, I §89). If the child were able to provide for himself, was his claim extinguished? And if the claim were to the parent's property when he died, should this limit the parent's power of disposal before his death? Locke was quite clear that other individuals should take account of the children's claims on a parent's property – so a conqueror in a just war might not deprive them of their parent's property, even if he might deprive the parent of life itself (II §183). A strong interpretation of the right to inherit would, therefore, constrain both the present possessor and others in his generation.

The other form of justification for inheritance is quite different. While the Lockean view seems to limit the powers of present owners, the justifications for the power of bequest treat that power as a reasonable extension of, or analogy to, the power that a present holder should be allowed. The power to bequeath is added to the rights of the owner by treating another right as established and then arguing for the similarity between that right and the right of bequest. The usual starting point is the right to transfer property *inter vivos*. It is then held that there is no moral difference betweeen such disposal in the owner's lifetime and his disposal by will after his death. The argument treats the parallel between *inter vivos* transfer and bequest as a justification for the latter, if the former is assumed.

Of course, the extent of the power of bequest thus justified could be no greater than the extent of the right to alienate.

Another version of the justification of the power of bequest has exactly the same logical structure but begins instead from the right to destroy property. In one way, this is merely a different level of justification to that just considered, because it could equally well be used to argue for the right of transfer *inter vivos*, the premise of the previous justification. Since an owner may legitimately destroy his property, the argument goes, he can surely transfer it to others, either in his lifetime or at his death. With both these arguments in favour of a right of bequest, a conclusion is drawn from the assertion of a right which is taken to be established – the right to destroy one's property, or the right to transfer it *inter vivos*. Counter-arguments, clearly, are of three kinds: those that deny the premise and therefore the conclusion; those that deny that the conclusion follows from the premise; and those that accept the argument, but adduce countervailing considerations.

The premise may be challenged because the owner's right to destroy his goods is too loosely specified. The central characteristic of property is that it regulates the use of resources, and anyone who uses a resource may ultimately destroy it. For most resources repeated use leads to uselessness, whether the resource be the jurisprudential toothbrush or a car engine or a mineral resource like coal or oil. But there is still a difference between a right to destroy a resource through use and a right to destroy useful property. The first form of destruction is often inevitable, while the second is not. If the rationale of property is to enable resources to be used, then unnecessary destruction is discountenanced by the very foundations of the theory. Hence Locke argued in favour of appropriation which would allow individuals (within families) to make use of God's gift, but specifically rejected appropriation which led to waste caused by unused resources spoiling in the possession of the appropriator. He also regarded a monetised exchange economy as an advantage in reducing the prospects of resources wasting, both because waste in possession would be avoidable by transfer and because such an economy encouraged the exploitation of resources. Although Locke's rationale for property is that the gift should be used, this certainly did not extend to wilful destruction.

Two points may be made about this approach. First, as we shall see in more detail shortly, avoiding waste or spoilage is for Locke a duty, and this duty may entail a right of transfer. Secondly, although it may be easy enough to distinguish between wilful destruction of a useful resource and destroying something through using it, there are many cases in which the elasticity in the notion of 'use' will cause problems. For example, stocks of oil are finite, but oil does not spoil (in Locke's terminology) in the same way that strawberries do. If someone picked strawberries and allowed them to rot, he would have offended against Locke's specification of legitimate appropriation. If the resource is oil, there will never be this sort of spoilage; but there may well be great wastefulness in its use. Like all fuels, oil can be used more or less efficiently, and inefficient use is unnecessarily wasteful. If we take seriously the idea that property is to make resources useful and avoid waste, then, we shall certainly want to rule out wilful destruction, but we may also be committed by our understanding of 'waste' to circumscribe the *way* in which resources are used as well. If the rationale of property is to avoid waste, a right to destroy one's property 'unnecessarily' could not be countenanced.

Nevertheless, the implications which may be drawn from a Lockean concern with use provide an alternative grounding for the right of transfer. The argument for bequest under consideration holds that the right to destroy property would legitimise a right of transfer and a right of bequest, because the owner is using a 'lesser' power in the latter two cases. The counter on Lockean grounds is that no such right of destruction exists. But the Lockean case places a duty on individuals to avoid waste. *If* only a right of transfer could avoid unnecessary spoilage and waste, then the duty to avoid spoilage requires such a right to be recognised. As we have seen, it is precisely this consequence of efficient use of resources which is used by the economic approach to property rights to validate their content.

Even if a right of transfer is regarded as established, it is possible to deny that it justifies a right of bequest by rejecting the claim that an *inter vivos* transfer and testamentary disposition have the same moral status. A testament is a contingent transfer, in the sense that the transfer is effected only on the death of the testator, and it may be regarded as stating what a person would wish to do by his living will before he died, if he could be certain when that event was to occur. Both the testament and an *inter vivos* transfer (by gift, sale and so on) express the will of the person with property; but that will exists before, during and (usually) after an *inter vivos* transfer, but only before a bequest. A bequest in this sense does not deprive the testator of anything. So 'respecting a person's will' in one case refers to the will of a living person, and in the other to a dead one. One justification for the right of bequest suggests that the right corresponds to an obligation on those left behind to respect the will of the dead person. The objection is that the deceased's will does not exist in the relevant sense. Whichever way the question is resolved, the right of bequest allegedly supported by an argument from a right of *inter vivos* transfer could not be more extensive than the latter.

Adam Smith, we may recall, found the notion of bequest puzzling, because, it was 'not at all necessary to property' (1978, p.309). He explained it – rather than justified it – as a consequence of the sentiment of association between property and its deceased owner (1978, p.38f, cf. 1853). Although bequest was, he thought, a late development, it was an extension of property, and entail was the greatest extension of all. Technically, entailment restricted the class of possible heirs to property, so it presupposed a power of bequest for at least the person who entailed his property. Considerable doubt was expressed about the desirability of allowing entailment, which we may briefly examine as it will connect our discussion of inheritance with problems of inter-generational justice (Thirsk, 1976).

The devices invented by lawyers advising clients who were attempting to entail property, and used by those trying to 'break' the entail, became extremely complex (Simpson, 1961, p.186). Nevertheless, the general problem is accessible without technicality. Let us suppose that Greenacre has left his estate in tail to his first-born male successors, and his own first-born son, Greenacre II, has duly inherited. If the terms of Greenacre's will bind Greenacre II, he will be required to leave the estate to his own first-born son. Under these circumstances, Greenacre II has much more limited powers to dispose of his property than his father had. It is this which occasioned the debate as to how far a testator should be allowed to reach into the future. If the right of bequest is to be grounded in a right of *inter vivos* transfer, the rules governing alienability and inheritance should be consistent. For example, could a living person 'reach into the future' by setting up a trust in his lifetime for the benefit of specific persons? The problem of 'balancing' the powers of bequest and alienation between generations are considerable. In our example, Greenacre II cannot exercise the same choices in his will as Greenacre. Moreover, if he is committed to handing on the estate to his own first-born son, he will be debarred from alienating it in his lifetime. (We have already seen that a strong interpretation of a right to inherit will truncate alienability.) Greenacre II's inability to alienate was the ground of Adam Smith's (1976, pp.382–6) objection to the practice – it kept land away from the market and reduced incentives to farm efficiently – but the objection can also be stated in terms of justice between generations: inheritance institutions should allow each present holder the same powers of disposal. So even if a person is allowed to specify what should happen to his property at his own death, he should not be able to reach into the future in such a way as to constrain the same power when his property has come into the hands of his successors. The debate about the desirability of entail again draws attention to the special status of land. The regulation of inheritance is merely one implication for property institutions which may be drawn from requirments of intergenerational justice which we shall look at more closely later in this chapter.

Another approach to inheritance is provided by theorists who associate private property with the right of personality – of whom we took Hegel as an example. The idealist argument that property is an expression of personality has been applied to the family unit as well as to the individual. Green (1931, pp.222–3) argued that because provision for the future is an expression and development of the responsibility of an individual for his family, it would be wrong to limit the provision an individual made for his future. Because it would be wrong to impose such a limitation, it would also be wrong to limit the provision an individual made for his children, since they are part of his provision for his future. For this reason, Green concluded, the amount of property which children should be allowed to receive by inheritance should not be stinted. In any case, he revealingly added, it would be improper to remove a father's discretion in distributing his property, because he could then take no account of faults like idleness, extravagance and lack of dutifulness. (Green was less certain about regulating the inheritance of land.)

This argument moves swiftly from the impropriety of limiting a man's provision for his future to the desirability of a power of bequest. It is not altogether clear whether the primary right Green wishes to establish is the right to bequeath, or the right to inherit – whether it would be wrong to limit what the father may choose to give, or wrong to limit what the children may receive. The contribution of the right of bequest to the father's authority suggests the former. Although he worried about the consequences of allowing this power – particularly for inequality and the possible exclusion of some persons from propertied status – Green ultimately defended it as allowing for the expression of personality and responsibility towards children. He seems to have wanted to balance the children's claims on the parent with the parent's discrimination in leaving his property to those most worthy to receive it. Only a small shift in the balancing of these considerations would lead to a justification of the right to inherit, rather than the right to bequeath, just as a rather greater concern with the inequality resulting from familial inheritance might truncate the right of bequest. Green's argument, it should be noted, appears to establish that if a person has children he should be allowed to determine their allotments of his property; it has nothing to say about the position of the childless, and provides no justification for a person to bequeath his property out of his family.

Green's concern is both to argue against the limitation of the size of a bequest, and the limitation of the amount any child might receive. In most countries in the contemporary world, duties are levied on the estate of a deceased person which reduce the amount available for disposal by bequest. Apart from the obvious use of such duties to raise revenue, it is often held that they reduce the perpetuation of inequality. In this context a proposal put forward by John Stuart Mill (1865, p.139) is of some interest. Mill shared the concern that unregulated inheritance would contribute to the maintenance or exacerbation of inequalities. But he proposed not a tax on the estate of the deceased person, but a limit on the amount any beneficiary might receive. This would encourage, if not require, the testator to disperse his wealth, and provides an example of an attempt to balance the right of bequest and a concern with its distributional consequences.

In their different ways, both Green and Mill were concerned with the development of responsibility. Mill's defence of freedom depends upon the contribution to that development which is made by the exercise of choice – an individual should be allowed to make decisions and bear the consequences, and this desirable exercise of choice extends to a plan of life or lifestyle which is his own (Halliday, 1976, pp.122–5; Ryan, 1974, pp.140–3; Ten, 1980, pp.144–73). That an individual should bear the consequences of his decisions is desirable for his own learning and so that he may provide an example to others. Green supposes that a process of development of personality occurs in the execution of a rational plan of life, a plan which includes family commitments and provision for children. A more recent philosophy which gives prominence to a plan of life has been developed by John Rawls, in *A Theory of Justice*. Rawls (1973, p.408) 'adapts' 'Royce's thought that a person may be regarded as a human life lived according to a plan'. Rawls is concerned to determine the formal characteristics of a rational plan of life, and the nature of the 'goods' necessary to pursue any such plan.

Private property has been valued because it provides a sphere in which an individual can pursue his plan or express his development, providing control over resources to accompany the fulfilment of his purposes. But Rawls, J. S. Mill and Green are not equally strong adherents of private property, despite a shared commitment to the value of self-chosen lifestyles and to the pursuit of plans of life. Mill (Schwartz, 1972, pp.153–92) was far more sympathetic to socialism, in the sense of common ownership of the productive resources, than Green, and Rawls (1972, p.280) does not suppose that either socialism or a private property market economy is uniquely required by his conception of the person or of the just society. The logical structure of the difficulties faced by a theorist committed to providing individuals with the opportunity to execute a plan of life will be familiar from our discussion of control over productive activity (Chapter 5). Hegel's notion that the assertion of the 'right of personality' required private property in which the will was externalised was extended in Green's similar idea that property was to provide the means to pursue a plan of life, to the conclusion that neither accumulation nor bequest should be subject to limitation. But both Hegel and Green were sensitive to the distributional problem, the danger of propertyless persons. Obviously, while the benefits of individual control over resources may be emphasised by those seeking to facilitate the execution of a plan of life, extensive control may deprive others of similar opportunities. Just as allowing one owner to entail his estate deprives his successors of as great a power of alienation and bequest as he exercised, and therefore leads to inequality in the control over resources through time, so allowing one individual the maximum control over resources to help him pursue his plan of life may deprive others of the same capacity. In this sense, the choice is between equal but limited powers, and extended powers with unequal results. Green seems to have favoured the latter, but J. S. Mill and Rawls give more weight to the distributional problem.

One version of the notion that property is part of the framework of a 'plan of life' has been integrated with the 'incentive argument' discussed in Chapter 5. According to that view, the secure enjoyment of property is an incentive necessary to overcome the disutility of labour. If this secure enjoyment is extended to cover provision for children, an argument in support of inheritance may be generated. It suggests that a person works in order to accumulate property not only for himself, but also for his children, and that inability to transmit property would weaken the incentive otherwise offered. It is sometimes asserted, for example, that a person would simply expend his resources on a comfortable life if he were not able to transmit them to his posterity, but the prospect of enhancing the lives of the next generation leads to greater exertions than would otherwise be forthcoming. Of course, the threat of disinheritance may provide the child with an incentive to comply with the parents' wishes about his behaviour – whatever they might be. Logically this argument is not restricted to transmission of property to the children of the testator, unless is it assumed that it is only the welfare of children which provides the necessary incentive. The incentive to accumulate provided by the power of testament is also presented as a disincentive to wasteful consumption. A common argument against the imposition of taxation on the estate of a deceased person holds that such consumption is the undesirable consequence of reducing the incentive to accumulate.

The inheritance of property has usually been thought of as a matter of the transmission of property from parents to children, and we have been anxious to point out that the logical implications of justifying this practice from a right to inherit and from a right to bequeath are quite different. We have also noticed that Green's argument, justifying a parental power to vary the quantities of property received by different children, tries to combine a right to receive property with some measure of parental discretion. The arguments which are not so tightly based on the transmission of property to children rely upon the incentive to accumulate (although even here the welfare of children may be treated as the strongest incentive) and more generally on the alleged analogy between a right to bequeath property and a right to transfer it or destroy it. We have seen that such an argument may be challenged first, because the right to destroy property is denied; and secondly, on the grounds that there is a moral difference between transfer *inter vivos* and bequest. Finally, even if a right of bequest is granted, it may be limited by concern with its distributional consequences or other countervailing considerations. Obviously, to the extent that inheritance is conceived to pass property between generations, it is crucial in any discussion of intergenerational justice, a topic looked at later in this chapter. Property has a role in linking generations, and providing for social stability through time, but this role depends partly on its contribution to the provision of a stable framework for action, an aspect discussed in the next section.

Property, stability and continuity

A core idea in the liberal concept of ownership is that the interest of an owner is terminable only by his own decision. Although Honoré included 'liability to execution' as an incident of that ownership, this may be seen as a requirement protecting other owners from termination beyond their control, rather than as a limitation of the core idea. The idea that persons should not be divested of their property by state action has also been central to the liberal political tradition, leading to a requirement that consent must be forthcoming, in Locke, and to doubts about extending the franchise to the poor. The proper limits of state action raise fundamental questions in political philosophy which obviously cannot be treated here. Nevertheless, it is worth noticing the association between property and stability which has informed writers with very different political persuasions. Ownership is terminable by the decision of the owner, and his interest is protected in various ways by the legal system. Clearly the protection could disappear if the state and its legal system collapsed, and the property rules were disregarded; but a general uncertainty has been expressed about the legitimacy of changing the property rules or depriving individuals of property which they had expected to enjoy. Two examples will illustrate this point.

Burke's political philosophy gave him many reasons to disfavour the influence of the so-called court party in the governance of the nation's affairs. One of the causes of that influence was crown patronage, the distribution of offices to favoured individuals who derived benefit from holding them. These 'offices' were in the sovereign's gift, and within the classification of property which the common law had adopted they were to be counted as real property. To reform government in such a way that these offices would be abolished would therefore deprive persons of property, and Burke was strongly attached to security of property for reasons we shall encounter in the next section. He drew the logical conclusion that these offices should not be simply abolished: rather reform would have to be delayed until the property interests of present holders expired (Burke, 1906, pp.356–7; Finer, 1952).

A second example is provided by the utilitarian concern with expectations. The Benthamite utilitarians recognised that existing property rules, especially with regard to inheritance, were not entirely desirable. But they also thought that to change these rules by a law of immediate application would frustrate the justified expectations of existing potential heirs. They therefore distinguished between an existing expectation and a future time when a change in the law would prevent the expectation arising. Bentham (1911, p.122) was only happy to use the law to produce a more equal distribution of property when the deceased was not only without a spouse, but childless and intestate as well. Property rules could therefore be used to interfere with the distribution of property only in a limited number of cases, where security was not endangered (1911, p.143). An important component of security was the absence of frustrated expectations (Long, 1979, p.226).

These are merely two examples of the way in which theorists have entertained doubts about the desirability of interfering with property, and they are obviously connected with the view that ownership gives an individual control over resources, which he should be justifiably confident will extend through time. It has seemed to many supporters of private property that even changes which they desired should proceed slowly, if they are to be consistent with the core idea that property distributes exclusive control over things through time.

The title of an owner is, in the standard case, without temporal limit. Nevertheless, societies find it convenient to have rules which relate title to the passage of time. Two examples are prescription, which founds a title in the uninterrupted enjoyment of property over a specified period, and rules regulating the transfer of title after a certain time has elapsed, as in provisions that property which has been lost and found, if not claimed by its original owner, will become the property of the finder after a certain time has elapsed. Both the origin and loss of title are often specified by reference to a period of time designed to ensure that no valued rights are neglected. Hence an owner who has not claimed his found property within a certain time is conceived to have abandoned it, while prescription respects a long and uninterrupted use of property.

A simple example of a prescriptive right may be taken from rights of way in England. It is possible to establish such a right over land by demonstrating that, over a particular period, this route has been available and that it has been used without interruption by anyone who might technically have the right to prevent passage. Such a prescriptive right may be regarded positively and negatively: on the positive side, it appears as though a new right has been acquired over land when the right of way is established, while negatively someone has lost the right of exclusion because he has chosen, over a long period, not to exercise it. There are still examples of places where a path usually available to the public is blocked on one day of the year, to rebut the claim of uninterrupted use. If the right of exclusion were not so exercised, a right of way might be created prescriptively, and the existing right of exclusion would disappear because of disuse. Rules governing the origin of title through prescription obviously require some specification of the time through which a particular state of affairs has existed, and this is usually a fairly long period, to ensure that no valued right is lost and to demonstrate the utility of the 'new' right.

While it is clear that private property systems will require rules to fill in the gaps, to enable it to be determined when property has been abandoned, and if it has what is to happen to it, it is difficult to imagine that prescription could provide much of a basis for the system of property as a whole. If it is important to know who has title to particular property, the precise formulation of the rule may be a matter of some indifference. Just as it is more important that everyone should drive on the same side of the road than that it be the left or the right, so it may well be more important to know whose responsibility particular property is (under a private property system) than to decide whether (for example) a finder acquires property after three months or a year (cf. Smith, 1978, pp.32–7).

Intergenerational justice

The attention which intergenerational justice is presently receiving is novel, although the problem it poses is not (Parfit, 1984). In its usual formulation, the problem is couched with an eye to the future. Brian Barry, for example, asks:

> 'what if anything [do] those alive at any given time owe their descendants, whether in the form of positive efforts (e.g. investment in capital goods) or in the form of forbearance from possible actions (e.g. those causing irreversible damage to the natural environment)?' (1977, p.268)

In the context of theories of property, and of many social attitudes towards it, we might reformulate this question to include an eye on the past: what, if anything, do those alive at time t owe to their predecessors? We have seen that one argument for inheritance requires us to respect the will of the deceased – the right of bequest corresponds to an obligation on successors to carry out the wishes of a person. In general, then, the issue which will be immediately raised when we consider the different time-spans of natural persons, resources, and legal titles is what obligations (whether legal or moral) should persons be conceived to have when dealing with property, which in a broad sense they have received from their forbears and which they will leave to their successors. This problem has become more pressing in the contemporary world partly as a consequence of the recognition of the exhaustible nature of many resources, and partly because future population seems increasingly to be under the control of the present generation. Although Barry addressed himself to the requirements of intergenerational justice as a whole, and not to property in particular, the conclusion of his essay is highly pertinent to our concerns:

> '. . . I conclude that those who say we need a "new ethic" are in fact

right. It . . . should surely as a minimum include the notion that those alive at any time are custodians rather than owners of the planet, and ought to pass it on in at least no worse shape than they found it in.' (1977, p.284)

Theories of justice may be derived from many sources or varieties of moral theory. For example, utilitarianism, Rawlsian contractarianism and Nozickian entitlement theory all put forward theories about what justice consists in. Obviously, the problem of justice between generations is but a part of the problem of explaining the nature of justice, or of the just society. Theories of justice are concerned with the consideration due to persons, and with the reference group of persons who are to be considered. We shall shortly examine both the problem of the reference group and a number of recent ideas about justice between generations applied to property. First we may note how Barry's conclusion may be connected to aspects of property we have already discussed. The notion that any generation should not do as it likes with resources, but rather should act as custodian of what it receives and pass it on in at least as good condition, links up with several issues. First, it brings to mind Locke's constraint on original appropriation, that enough and as good be left for others, and Nozick's interpretation of the Lockean proviso, that the position of others should not be worsened by an act of appropriation. The central issue is, which others? Those who happen to be alive at the time, or those who (may) come after? Another way of expressing Barry's minimum condition is to say that a subsequent generation should be no worse off because of the use of resources made by any particular living population, while Locke's condition is that others should be left enough and as good after an act of appropriation for use. An optimistic view holds that the market system is capable of achieving this result. Nozick, we saw, is explicit that a free-market system will not violate the Lockean proviso. He also alleges that one of the 'familiar social considerations favoring private property' is that 'it protects future persons by leading some to hold back resources from current consumption for future markets' (1974, p.177). However, as Barry points out, the entitlement theory apparently allows a present owner to destroy his goods if he wishes (1977, p.273), so this provision is at best a possibility and certainly is not guaranteed within the theory. Nozick's position is that while there is no obligation to provide for future generations, it is a desirable empirical characteristic of free-market private-property regimes that some such provision sometimes happens.

A second link is to the notion of entail. The entailed estate, we saw, may limit the present holder's rights over it to a large extent, and give rise to the objection that powers of disposal are unequally distributed between persons over time. If we wish to provide for future generations, however, especially fairly remote generations, such restrictions may be justified. Barry suggests that in preserving capital over a long period we are discouraged by the fact that:

> 'there is no way in which we can be confident that our efforts will have any net effect because everything depends on the behaviour of the intervening generations, whom we have no way of binding.' (1977, p.276)

Although 'entail' referred to particular families and specific individuals, rather than indeterminate 'generations', the whole motive behind it was to bind present possessors to pass on intact to their descendants the estate which they themselves had inherited. Indeed, we are told that moral scruple often prevented such a possessor breaking the entail, even when it was legally possible:

> '. . . people felt conscientious objections about devising freely land acquired as patrimony, and the gravest doubt of all surrounded their moral right to cut off an entail.' (Thirsk, 1969, p.365)

While it is of course true that the existence of a legal mechanism for entailing property will not guarantee that the entails will be preserved, especially in the remote future, the central idea of entailment is to provide the security the absence of which Barry regards as a significant disincentive to our recognition of any obligation to future inhabitants of our planet.

A third link is to Burke's vision of social life as a contract between generations. One argument for private property which we have encountered is that it provides the material dimension to a planned life in which projects can be realised against some background security. Burke's image of society as a contract between generations exhibits property, and land in particular, as a resource which ties together those temporally separated in a society's existence, binding them to a common way of life. This intergenerational contract of society is, of course, to be sharply distinguished from the individualistic social contract associated with rights theorists whom Burke deplored, and it is as much concerned with duties to predecessors as it is with duties to successors. For this reason, the notion of guardianship, of preserving a heritage intact, is crucial to it, and comes very close to Barry's minimum condition.

Burke's famous account of the contract between generations is given in his *Reflections on the Revolutions in France*:

'It is a partnership in all science; a partnership in all art; a partnership in every virtue, and in all perfection. As the ends of such a partnership cannot be obtained in many generations, it becomes a partnership not only between those living, but between those who are living, those who are dead, and those who are to be born.' (1910, p.93)

The transmission of property from one generation to the next was itself a manifestation of this contract, or partnership. Unfortunately, as Macpherson has pointed out, Burke did not give much guidance about the principles which would disclose the content of our obligations (Macpherson, 1980, p.46). Nevertheless, since Burke pursued an analogy between the inherited and prescriptive rights of Englishmen, and the mode of transmitting property, something may be inferred from obligations to respect the political liberties:

'You will observe, that from Magna Charta to the Declaration of Right, it has been the uniform policy of our constitution to claim and assert our rights as an *entailed inheritance* derived to us from our forefathers, and to be transmitted to our posterity, as an estate specially belonging to the people of this kingdom, without any reference whatever to any other more general or prior right.' (1910, p.31)

Entail is clearly welcomed as a means to preserve the inheritance intact.

The issues which arise from a consideration of justice between generations, in its implications for property, are these. First, do we

have obligations to our predecessors, our successors, or both? If we
do have any such obligations, what implications do they have for the
desirable structure of property rules? Even if we could agree on
principles which encapsulated the extent of our obligations,
something like Barry's minimum condition, there would remain a
great deal of dispute about the best means to fulfil the principles.
Some, like Nozick, would defend the capacity of the market system
and full powers of disposal of property, while others, like Burke,
would stress the need for self-conscious custodianship and self-
denial in the treatment of what had been inherited. The principles
specifying the obligations would have consequences both for rights
of transfer and rights of bequest or inheritance. For Nozick, the
owner's decision about what should happen to his property has the
same status during his life as in bequest (although since the right of
transfer is limited by the shadow of the Lockean proviso, the right of
bequest is presumably so limited as well). He thinks that a full
market will not violate that proviso, and that private property
systems encourage some benefit for future generations, although he
does not recognise an *obligation* on the living to secure this result.
By contrast, Burke held that we must treat our property (and its
distribution) with some reverence, bestowing sufficient care on it to
be able to transmit it in at least as good condition:

> 'The power of perpetuating property in our families is one of the
> valuable and interesting circumstances belonging to it, and that
> which tends the most to the perpetuation of society itself. It
> makes our weakness subservient to our virtue; it grafts
> benevolence even upon avarice. The possessors of family wealth,
> and of the distinction which attends hereditary possession (as
> most concerned in it), are the natural securities for this
> transmission.' (1910, p.49)

While the perpetuation of state and society should be modelled
on the transmission of property, so the abuse of the 'inherited state'
discloses what would be an abuse of property:

> 'But one of the first and most leading principles on which the
> commonwealth and the laws are consecrated, is lest the temporary
> possessors and life-renters in it, unmindful of what they have
> received from their ancestors, or of what is due to their posterity,

should act as if they were the entire masters; that they should not think it among their rights to cut off the entail, or commit waste on the inheritance, by destroying at their pleasure the whole fabric of their society; hazarding to leave to those who come after them a ruin instead of an habitation – and teaching these successors as little to respect their contrivances, as they had themselves respected the institutions of their forefathers.' (1910, pp.91–2)

The consequence of accepting Burke's notion of proper provision for future generations is of course quite different from the operation of a free market and a right of destruction licensed, according to Nozick, by the entitlement theory. So their conclusions may be initially contrasted as follows. Burke is quite clear that an obligation to future (and past) generations exists, and that it is to be discharged by the proper guardianship of a social inheritance embodied in property and in other institutions which should be modelled on it. Nozick does not accept an obligation to future generations which would limit a present owner's disposal of his property.

Our third author, Rawls, accepts that there is some obligation in a just society to provide for future generations, which is defined by (what he calls) the just savings principle. His proposal for deriving this principle has been the subject of some criticism, but in any case the politico-economic system which will put the just savings rate into effect is not determinable simply from knowledge of the rate. Rawls treats that question, an answer to which would reveal the implications of the just savings rate for property institutions, as an open-ended empirical issue, so although there is an obligation to future generations, the best (property) regime to discharge it is unsettled. A basic feature of social systems, he says:

'. . . is the extent to which the market is used to decide the rate of saving and the direction of investment, as well as the fraction of national wealth devoted to conservation and the elimination or irremediable injuries to the welfare of future generations. Here there are a number of possibilities. A collective decision may determine the rate of saving while the direction of investment is left to individual firms competing for funds. In both a private-property as well as in a socialist society great concern may be expressed for preventing irreversible damages and for husbanding natural resources and preserving the environment. But again either one may do rather badly.' (1972, p.271)

Although he treats the implementation of the just savings rate with some agnosticism, Rawls does have an account of why justice requires this concern for future generations, and an account of the principles which could lead to the determination of the desirable rate. He rejects the utilitarian proposal, of maximizing total utility, because it could place unreasonable burdens on poor generations to advantage subsequent and richer ones. His own 'contractarian' solution is that the just rate would be agreed by a set of individuals who did not know which generation they (collectively) belonged to (and were ignorant about some other matters as well). There is a large literature on Rawls' theory which may be consulted by anyone who wishes to place the just savings rate in its proper context (Daniels, 1975; Barry, 1973), but it is noteworthy that if the contractarian proposal could successfully disclose a just savings rate it would give a more definite content to Burke's idea that we should deny ourselves complete mastery over property, avoid waste and preserve our inheritance. In fact, the Rawlsian contract of justice is more than a little reminiscent of Burke's intergenerational contract:

> 'The process of accumulation, once it is begun and carried through, is to the good of all subsequent generations. Each passes on to the next a fair equivalent in real capital as defined by a just savings principle. [. . .] This equivalent is in return for what is received from previous generations that enables the later ones to enjoy a better life in a more just society.' (1972, p.288)

Until some specification of what form of society is necessary to implement the rate can be made, however, the implications of this perspective for property regimes is undetermined.

It is regrettable but understandable that we do not find *both* a clear account of the nature of obligations to subsequent generations *and* a specification of the content of property rights in any one theory. Nozick is quite clear about the content of property rights on the entitlement theory, but he rejects any obligations to future generations. Nozick does propose a principle of rectification, specifying how an unjust appropriation or transfer should be corrected, but it is very difficult to see how it could be applied to present holdings of property given our knowledge of the history of appropriation. Rawls deduces the existence of such obligations from the nature of justice, but is not committed to any particular social system to realise them. Barry accepts the obligations, but is able to specify only the minimum condition that each generation should pass on the planet in at least as good condition as it found it – so that any one generation should regard itself as custodians of resources, not as owners entitled to do as they please. Burke emphasises a similar notion of custody, extolling the virtues of entailed inheritance as a means to put it into effect. Our next reference to a theory of intergenerational justice which has consequences for property provides an example of precision with respect to both the nature of the obligations and the content of property rights, but one which would be difficult to implement in practice.

In a connected series of articles, Hillel Steiner has developed a particular view of rights and the importance of titles to property within that conception (1977a; 1977b; 1981; 1982; 1984). He has been interested in the logical characteristics of a compossible set of rights, a set of rights, that is, which could be exercised without conflict with other rights (1977a). On traditional understandings of rights, the exercise of one person's right could easily conflict with another person's – for example, if two people simultaneously try to exercise a right to free speech in precisely the same part of public space. According to Steiner's view, a compossible set of rights is necessarily a set of rights which are (or are reducible to) titles to objects rather than entitlements to pursue (or have others refrain from pursuing) certain specified kinds of intention (1984, p.230). A compossible set of rights, therefore, must be a set of property rights, consisting in (exclusive) titles to objects. If we now suppose the existence of natural rights, that is, rights attributable to individuals whoever they are and in whatever generation they are born, we may ask what a compossible set of natural rights would be like. Steiner's own view is that, if there are any natural rights, the natural right to the means of production must be among them (1977b). The hypothetical phrasing of the argument follows H. L. A. Hart (1955), who suggested in a famous essay that if there are any natural rights, the right to equal liberty must be among them. The conclusion of Steiner's argument has strong implications for intergenerational justice. It requires us to suppose that at time t there is a stock of means of production to which everyone in the existing population has a right. If the population changes, or the stock of productive resources changes, then the equation will be altered. Each individual has a right to Z/n means of production, where Z is the total stock and n is the population. As Steiner himself noted, it is not easy to imagine an institutional embodiment of this prescription. He specified this formula as the necessary consequence of accepting both natural rights and the demands of compossibility. We shall return to the problem of ascribing natural rights shortly. We may note here that property rights are uniquely important in Steiner's attempt to design a set of compossible rights, because they, unlike rights to perform specified intentional actions, hold out some hope of success. The significance of this result depends on how highly the absence of conflict of rights is valued.

Bruce Ackerman (1980) has derived a similar result from a different argument. Steiner suggests that each individual is entitled to Z/n means of production; Ackerman proposes a formula to work out the justifiable endowment (in *per capita* capital stock) of members of a second generation in an ideal society. He explores the issue of intergenerational justice through an imagined dialogue between individuals who are constrained by certain principles governing 'power talk' (1980, p.8). The device of dialogue is used throughout *Social Justice in the Liberal State* to establish the requirements of justice, and it is to be contrasted with contractarian, utilitarian and historical approaches. According to Ackerman, if the persons in the first generation of the ideal world decide to have children, then

'each child is entitled to an endowment that is no worse than:
1. that provided to any of his age-mates.
2. that obtained by any older citizen with whom the younger citizen can converse.' (1980, p.217)

This principle obviously leaves the source of the endowment which the child receives to be determined. Clearly it would severely constrain conventional testamentary disposition, but it would also provide a justification for inheritance. Underlying the principle is a notion of trusteeship – that the next generation is entitled to as great an initial endowment as the present one, but has no claim to receive more. It is this principle which is applied to the *per capita* capital stock.

It should be noted that the device of dialogue constrains the comparison between generations which the theory accommodates

(1980, p.222). We recall that Barry drew attention to the problem of provision for *distant* generations, that we do not know how the intervening generations will behave, while dialogue presupposes the contemporary existence of persons of different ages. Again, Barry's notion of trusteeship, that the planet should be passed on in at least as good condition as it was received, is not unpacked into *individual* endowments, as Ackerman's is.

There is a problem facing all attempts to provide a justification for a property system, namely the reference group of persons whose claims are to be considered. A natural rights theory, for example, ascribes rights to persons whoever they are and whenever they are born. In the modern world, individuals are subject to different jurisdictions, which may interfere with the realisation of intragenerational justice. Additionally, of course, they are temporally separated, and this raises the problem of intergenerational justice with which we have been concerned. We may now explore the connection between these two problems of jurisdictional and temporal separation a little further.

There is no world government of which all persons are subjects, and declarations of rights which claim to have universal applicability depend for their implementation on ratification by particular states. Arguments about justice, intergenerational justice and therefore about the proper behaviour of existing property-holders, may well specify moral requirements to be met by particular groups which are not identical with members of particular states. For example, a rigorous utilitarian who aims to maximise average utility need not confine his concerns to persons who live under the same jurisdiction as himself – except on the pragmatic grounds that his calculations are thereby simplified and that their position is more immediate to him. Similarly, theories of intergenerational justice have implications for how we should treat resources, given that other persons will come after us. But these subsequent persons are not all members of our society, even though we might endeavour to make the rules of our society consistent with the demands of intergenerational justice. So such theories of justice may call upon us to recognise obligations which, in the nature of the case, cannot be given complete expression within a particular legal system.

In this respect we may generalise a point made by Nozick (1974, p.178). It is not only defenders of private property, he says, who need a justification of exclusion of other persons from control over resources. Those who support common property must also show why it is legitimate for the commoners to exclude non-commoners. This is obviously correct. The generalisation is that a discussion of the way in which property is treated *within* a decision-making unit like a state should not neglect the possible claims of those currently living outside it, for citizens collectively regulate access to 'their' property through the state's jurisdiction. This explains why theories of property are often embedded in grander theories of political organisation, and attempts to integrate discussion of the legitimacy of political power with the legitimacy of property. As we saw in Chapter 3 and Chapter 5, this is likely to be an especially difficult problem for a natural rights theorist, since a natural right is attributable to an individual whatever generation or decision-making unit he finds himself in, and the structure of the theory should not foreclose the enjoyment of those rights by persons other than those who are first to exercise them, whether or not the others are in the same generation.

Anarchy, State and Utopia is a clear example of the attempt to make the account of legitimate property rights consistent with a theory of the limits of legitimate state power. One advantage which might be claimed for the historical entitlement theory of holdings is that it does not run into problems when the reference group to whom it is applied alters. That is, if a set of holdings has arisen in accordance with the theory in Erewhon, and a similarly legitimate set of holdings has emerged in Atlantis, then the holdings will remain 'just' when a reference group which combines the populations of those two countries is used. This is not true of a distributive theory which aims for distribution of resources according to (let us say) need. Distribution may meet the claims of justice within Erewhon, and Atlantis, given what there is to distribute: but if the two societies are combined, a redistribution will almost certainly be necessary to preserve the fit between need and holdings. In this respect Nozick's theory aims to integrate the account of legitimate property rights with the legitimacy of the decision-making unit, through his account of historical entitlement (1974, p.209).

The same ambition of making the theory of original entitlement and the theory of sovereignty consistent appears in *The Two Treatises*. Locke began by distinguishing property from political power, suggesting that Filmer had been in error when he assimilated them. Political power, for Locke, was legitimate only if those over whom it was exercised had consented to it, while property was legitimate if appropriation had occurred in accordance with the laws of nature. Since political society was originally constituted by a number of men who had acquired property coming together to found it, the relationship between territory, jurisdiction and political authority, for *that* generation, was straightforward. The collective territory was pooled property over which the political association could claim jurisdiction, and no-one could become a member of the association without contributing his property, because the object of the commonwealth was to provide protection for it. Nor could anyone be divested of his property without his consent. Hence the story of the origins of property is linked to the story of the origins of political power and an assessment of the legitimacy of both. If the original appropriation were just, in accordance with the laws of nature, then those outside the community could have no cause to complain about the emergence of the political association. But matters are less simple when intergenerational considerations arise.

Once territory had been incorporated into a political society, it could not be withdrawn (1965, II §120). But children have a natural right to inherit, at least sufficient for subsistence, as we have seen Locke claim. Again, political authority is legitimate only if those over whom it is exercised have consented to it (II §195, §122). Locke has difficulties reconciling these ideas. He finally concluded that if a child wished to enjoy his inheritance, he must take it on the same terms as his father held it under – subjection to a particular political community (II §117). So the child, unlike the first founders, has a restricted choice about the political society, if not government, to which he is to give his political allegiance. If he is to inherit, he must accept a particular existing society. He can forsake his inheritance and try his luck elsewhere, but he cannot receive it without submission to the commonwealth. Locke's attempt to separate political power from property ultimately breaks down when the transmission of property becomes entangled with the transmission of political allegiance. This is because the state, its constituting territory and the property titles it guarantees exist before some of the persons who have claims on the property which it includes.

While the account of the legitimacy of property should be consistent with the account of the legitimacy of the political power which is to regulate it, it is no longer clear that all resources are adequately controlled by states. The activities of multinational and transnational companies disturb the simple picture by which property, citizens and jurisdiction are integrated. No doubt many features of these companies are novel, but the basic problem they pose for a simple picture of the legal control of property or resources is that explicit in Adam Smith's contrast between the landowner and the merchant. The multinational company is the merchant *par excellence*, whose allegiance to any particular community is contingent on market forces, and whose ability to switch resources between countries is an essential part of its ordinary operations. So while the traditional problem has been to show how property is related to state power, a new concern is with the limits on the autonomy of states. Just as such companies to some extent stand outside separate jurisdictions, so their capital is to some extent insulated, by stock markets, from the time-spans of individuals.

The problem of intergenerational justice which we have reviewed complicates attempts to show that any particular system of property is legitimate, because it moves beyond assessing that legitimacy with reference to a set of contemporaries and looks too at the location of that generation in the time dimension of social existence. It assesses the claims of those who have gone before and those who have yet to come, in addition to the claims of members of a particular generation. Inheritance is an obvious nexus for the issues which arise in this context. The problem may best be expressed by inverting Nozick's stricture against theories of distributive justice. They wrongly suppose, he suggests (1974, p.160), that things come into the world ready to be distributed to whomever the favoured theory regards as deserving; but, he holds, this is incorrect because things come into the world attached to persons who already have claims over them. The problem we have been discussing is the inverse of this. Persons are born into a world in which property is already attached to states, individuals and collectivities, and the question is what makes it legitimate to require these new arrivals to respect a division of property about which they were not consulted.

7 Conclusion

To understand an issue in political theory is to have an appreciation of disagreements, and ideally to move beyond such an appreciation to a resolution of the issue. This requires not only analysing the arguments put forward by the protagonists in any particular dispute, to assess their coherence, but also grasping the causes of the disagreement. In other words, we want to know not only *what* is contested, but also how it is possible for such contestation to arise. We have not directly addressed any of the methodological problems which are relevant to such a concern in this book, because the priority has been to lay out the disagreements. But we may conclude by reflecting on the kinds of issues we have encountered, paying attention to their more fundamental origins. We would expect, of course, that this would lead to some basic difficulties common to many areas of political theory. In this light it will be helpful to locate issues in the discussion of property within a wider context.

Chapter 2 addressed conceptual questions – what is 'property'? How is 'ownership' to be analysed? Since property and ownership are attributed to an assortment of agencies (such as corporations, individuals, the public), a full account requires an explication which will reveal the meaning of the concepts applied in these various ways. Such an account would show, for example, how 'individual ownership' and 'public property' are to be understood. A methodological question, (the proper response to which is certainly highly contested in political theory) is how such conceptual enquiry should be judged (e.g. Miller, 1983; Connolly, 1983, pp.213–47; Barry, 1965, pp.1–34). There is first the problem of deciding what standards of success are appropriate. For example, is the meaning of 'ownership' to be determined by reference to what is usually conveyed by the term, to the technical meaning to be found in law, or to some other standard? The second problem is whether conceptual elucidation necessarily invokes normative

179

commitments, or whether we can hope to provide an 'objective' account of the concept. Clearly, for terms which already have a normative dimension, or prescriptive implication, these are serious difficulties. They are exacerbated by the ambition of providing 'property', or a particular property system, with justification. The solution adopted in Chapter 3 was to provide an account of the formal characteristics of property, specifying both what a descriptive account would need to investigate and what a prescriptive account would need to fill in and justify. The framework developed to provide this formal characterisation revealed that 'property' is capable of greaty variety and complexity, and so an attempt to provide a full description of any particular property system, or a complete justification of a favoured property system, would necessarily be highly elaborate.

The capacity of property systems to exhibit great variety is also the cause of the difficulties encountered in Chapter 3, when we looked at some attempts to write about its history. Many of the changes in the organisation of social life may also be considered as alterations in property. But a history of property has to be selective about the changes which it treats as significant, and it has to provide an account which encompasses both practices and ideas. A concern with the history of property follows naturally enough from sensitivity to the variety of forms it can adopt. It also requires the theorist to explain how the history of property should be characterised, and what significance (if any) this history has for the desirability of property systems. We saw that most histories of property are embedded in some account of social organisation which has normative uses – this is quite plain in the Marxist account of modes of production, but also present in interpretations of Genesis and in Macpherson's attempt to locate the origins of 'the' modern concept of property. Obviously, a preliminary issue here is whether the history provided is accurate, and in particular whether the criteria used to isolate significant alterations in property are coherent and well chosen. A further issue is whether the history has any normative significance, and if so, what that is. There is bound to be a reciprocal connection between the historical and the conceptual enquiries: historical information exhibits the variety of forms which need to be accommodated by conceptual explication, while conceptual enquiry locates a particular modern understanding of property the 'development' of which the historical account attempts to trace. Hence we find disputes about the meaning attached to terms like *dominium* or 'property' by authors whom we seek to understand, whether they be medieval monks or seventeenth-century legal lexicographers. These disputes are partly about the evidence for any particular interpretation offered, but underlying them are methodological issues about the proper procedures to 'recover' meanings.

Chapters 4 and 5 dealt with the disputed connection between various forms of property, on the one side, and conceptions of liberty, power and labour on the other. Since 'liberty', in particular, may be understood in a number of different ways, we separated disputes which arise from alternative understandings of liberty from disputes about the consequences for property when there is a common understanding of that term. We discovered that a shared conception of liberty does not necessarily lead to a shared prescription about property. A part of the reason, we saw, was that assessments of the characteristics of social organisations like markets differ. Again, similar conclusions about property might be reached by those with rival understandings of liberty or the nature of work. Various conceptions of liberty and labour flow from alternative accounts of 'human nature', and rival assessments of what man is capable of achieving. Furthermore, any single conception of liberty or labour requires many other assumptions to be introduced before it generates any particular conclusions about property. These assumptions will necessarily include assessments of economic systems. But the way in which such systems operate is itself historically variable, and it is important to draw out the economic system which a thinker envisages as consonant with his view of property.

Changes in the economic system, and the technology it employs, are part of the interpretations offered by histories of property. Economic developments also raise difficulties in contemporary political philosophy, because they highlight concern with intergenerational justice. The knowledge that our use of the world shapes the form in which subsequent generations receive it may have been with us throughout history, but our present awareness of the exhaustibility of resources relative to our level of use, and growing sensitivity to ecological damage and disaster, particularly in the light of rapid population growth, are relatively recent.

Less dramatically, new developments, even if foreseen, require continuing responsiveness if property is to fulfil our needs and purposes. For example, 'intellectual property' has become more important economically, because knowledge of processes and manufacturing techniques is a significant component of the ability to produce many 'goods'. At the same time, new technology is the source of difficulties for those anxious to maintain control over their intellectual products. Cassette machines are used to copy records, video machines to copy films and television programmes, and photocopying machines are used to reproduce the printed page. Again, great ingenuity is expended by individuals who are trying both to prevent and to make possible the duplication of computer software.

Many social developments may require us to think again about the structure of the property system. The most obvious are undoubtedly those connected with production. We saw that conclusions about the desirable system of property have been drawn from particular conceptions about work. Changes in the way production actually occurs may challenge us to think again about property relations. For example, most Western societies are now incapable of guaranteeing employment to all those who seek it, raising the immediate issue of the terms on which access to the means of production is to be secured. For example, a protracted dispute between the National Coal Board and the National Union of Mineworkers began in Britain in 1984. It turned on decisions to withdraw some mines from production. Should these decisions be made by assessing the physical exhaustion of pits, or their 'economic viability'? Again, technology has displaced labour in many productive activities, and some consumer goods are now built partially by robots. Clearly there is a world of difference between an economy of independent artisans and a modern high technology economy. New developments may undermine our assumptions about the compatibility between an existing property system and our normative commitments. Another example of social change is the shifting pattern of family life and with it the increasing irrelevance of some of the arguments encountered, especially about inheritance, to the lifestyles adopted in contemporary society.

We can isolate a number of problems underlying the attempt to provide coherence to the political theory of property. It will be worth considering the extent to which these problems are peculiar to property and the extent to which they are reflections of broader difficulties in political theory. These considerations will help to explain how the sort of contestation which we have reviewed in this book arises.

The first problem is the provision of conceptual clarity, the aspect of the political theory tackled in Chapter 2. This is certainly not a problem unique to 'property', because there are many concepts involved in political debate which are, on reflection, less clear than we might hope. Two obvious examples are 'power' and the 'public interest'. While 'property' is not unusual in demanding explication, there are two specific factors which add to our difficulties. These are first, the eclecticism of political theory combined with the existence of technical meanings of 'property' and 'ownership', and secondly, the dependence of most arguments about property on (other) values, like equality or liberty.

Political theory draws on many disciplines and therefore has to take account of the usages of those disciplines. 'Property' and 'ownership' may be approached through the concerns of law, economics, sociology and so on. This feature is obviously not peculiar to these concepts. The notion of 'rational action', for example, is employed in many fields of enquiry, and indeed is not understood in the same way by all investigators. In the case of 'property' and 'ownership' the dominant technical usage is legal. Again, the existence of technical meanings of the concepts employed in political theory is commonplace. 'Welfare', for example, is employed in a technical sense by economists.

The second factor in the difficulty of conceptual clarification is that much of the disagreement about property is a consequence of contested understandings of (other) values like 'liberty'. Theorists disagree about desirable property systems because they understand (other) values in conflicting ways. If we analyze these disagreements we may conclude that the focus of controversy is not 'property' itself, but some other normative commitment. So, although many disputes about property flow from other disagreements, which we have identified in the previous chapters, isolating the root of the issues is only a preliminary to investigating them. Other concepts share this feature. For example, some disagreement about the 'public interest' is a consequence of rival views of how individual interests should be analyzed. Often, in such cases, the fundamental dispute is about 'human nature', involving conflicting assessments of man's needs, purposes and potentialities.

This dispute, of course, has provided political theory with much of its richness and vitality, but also with its most intractable dilemmas.

The second problem we have encountered, in addition to this need for conceptual elucidation, is the historical specificity of many arguments about property. There are two aspects to this. First, the meaning of terminology changes. Secondly, the assumptions upon which an argument rests need to be drawn out because even if they were once appropriate they might no longer hold. For instance, it may well have been reasonable for Locke to suggest that the world contained many unused tracts of land (1965, II §121). But this seventeenth-century assumption is a good deal less plausible now, when states have established claims even to the inhospitable polar regions, and when we may need to determine whether titles to portions of other planets are to be admitted (McDougal, 1963). Once again, the historical specificity of assumptions embodied in complex arguments is not unique to disputes about property. Many claims about 'democracy' depend upon the size of the community thought to be capable of enjoying it, and it makes some difference that the population of Jefferson's America was 5.3 millions and the population of the contemporary United States over 226 millions.

One especially important aspect of the assumptions held by anyone writing about property is the organisation of economic activity he has knowledge of or envisages. Obviously, we cannot expect writers living several centuries before us to take account of the features of modern economic life. So we have to assess the coherence of a theory by reference to the economic system (we think) such writers envisaged when they put their arguments forward. But at the same time we cannot assume that *even if* the theory is convincing with reference to that economic system, it will be equally plausible when confronted by subsequent developments. Hodgskin's (1832) proposals for a society which recognised property in the product of a person's labour, for example, envisaged that producers are participants in a product market. Although we might be able to imagine such a society, it would clearly be very different from the one in which we now live.

A third problem also arises from the passage of time. This may be regarded generally as a difficulty generated by the dynamics of an institution like property. Instability in the system of property may undermine its rationale. Part of this is well expressed in Becker's (1977, pp.94–5) notion of self-defeatingness, and we have alluded to

T. H. Green's recognition of the problem already. The justification put forward for any favoured property system must be compatible with the consequences of instantiating that system over time. In Green's case, the justification for private property was that it allowed individuals to pursue a planned, moral life. Admitting the property rights which seemed necessary to secure that goal, however, also admitted the possibility that some persons would be deprived of the opportunity to lead such a life by the distribution of property which would result. We explored similar issues in relation to control over one's productive activity.

Clearly, there may well be instability in the distribution of many goods; the problem for justifications of property is not the instability *as such*, but rather the incompatibility between the rationale of property and the distribution achieved if it is admitted. For example, it is notoriously difficult to balance the liberty of different persons, to ensure that 'freedom for the pike' does not mean 'death for the minnows' (Berlin, 1969, p.124). But this distributional problem need not undermine the rationale for providing individuals with liberty. Many liberals would accept that unequal prosperity is a necessary consequence of admitting the freedom which they value. The point which worried Green combines our second problem of historical specificity with the danger of self-defeatingness. He was worried about the prospects for a propertyless proletariat. If a set of property rights and its attendant distribution of property under one system of production (which is consistent with the justification of property) may themselves lead to changes in the system of production, then self-defeatingness may work dynamically. For instance, even if a society of independent producers is uniquely capable of giving recognition to property in the product of labour, if that society is unstable and will lead to capitalism, the rationale for the preferred property system will disappear.

A fourth problem is that a justification for any favoured property system would have to be highly detailed, if it were sufficiently complete to be convincing. The complexity of argument required to produce such detail is an important reason for the occurrence of disputes about property. Since a multiplicity of assumptions, ideas and arguments is necessary to generate a specific conclusion, it may be challenged by a rejection of any of the elements in the case. The incentive argument provides a good example. This involves the claim that labour is a disutility; that individual reward is necessary to overcome that disutility; that property is an appropriate and necessary reward; and that such a system of incentives works to the general advantage. But, of course, all these elements in the case are disputable. Labour under appropriate conditions may be fulfilling, not a disutility. Rewards other than property, like honour and fame, may be adequate to call forth exertion, even if labour is unpleasant. And there may be no institutions capable of ensuring that such an incentive system does work to the general benefit.

It is also because of the multitude of joint assumptions necessary to draw a conclusion that we find similar premises leading to contradictory results, even if only one step in the argument has been changed. For example, two theorists who share a concern with an individual's control over his productive activity may disagree about how it should best be realised through the property system. One may hold that social control over joint production is required, and commit himself to collective property, while the other might maintain that independence necessitates private property appropriately distributed. This conflict itself could rest on a dispute about the stability of the distribution favoured by the second protagonist, perhaps because of disagreement about how markets operate over time.

Because a convincing account of the justification of property would have to be rather detailed, many arguments intended to establish the value of a favoured system of property in fact established rather less. For instance, Green's case for the legitimacy of inheritance asserts that children are part of a person's provision for the future, and that the parent should be able to discriminate between his offspring as to who is morally deserving, or worthy to receive his property. *Even if* this is a good argument for the familial transmission of property, it justifies neither transmission by the childless nor receipt of property by persons other than the children of the deceased. In this sense the conclusion of his argument has a more limited scope than he himself acknowledged.

The aim of many arguments about property is to begin with general considerations, such as justice or liberty, and then to move towards the justification of a detailed property system licensed by these considerations. Nevertheless this aim is frequently not realised. None of the theories of intergenerational justice which we looked at, for example, specified the content of property rights *and* the institutional structure consistent with the realisation of the obligations proposed. Rawls's theory of a just savings rate constrains the present generation for the sake of its successors, but his account leaves open the question of whether a socialist or private property system will be able better to fulfil this requirement. Answering this question would require a, great deal more (contestable) argument.

For all these reasons, then, we can see how the issues which surround the political theory of property arise. Whilst the range of argument may appear daunting, we should console ourselves by recognising that property systems are capable of great variety. Consequently, we do not have to make unconditional commitments to either private property or public property (however conceived). We may be prepared therefore to acknowledge the strength of particular arguments about the desirable character of property rights in limited fields. We may acknowledge that private property allows for the creation of privacy and the flowering of personality, but distinguish between personal and household property on the one side and productive resources on the other. Just because property is so central to social life, we must continue to attune our notions of legitimate property to our normative commitments, and to our experience of the consequences of existing property systems. The theorists examined in this book contribute to that enterprise, and there is much to be learned from them; but it is even more important that we apply insights gleaned from examining theories of property to the conditions of the world in which we live.

Guide to Further Reading

Theories of property have usually been advanced within a social or political theory with wider ambitions, and the range of considerations which have been brought to bear on the institution of property reflects the diversity of approaches to be found in the history of social theory. For this reason, two collections of essays which provide historical overviews are useful. Macpherson has extracted some important passages about property from a number of writers in *Property – Mainstream and Critical Positions* (1978), contributing an introduction and a stimulating concluding essay. The extracts will lead the reader back to the original works and the fuller context of the theories advanced. The other volume is edited by Parel and Flanagan (1979). *Theories of Property Aristotle to the Present* provides a good selection of interpretative essays, and although it is of course selective the volume does cover thinkers from Aristotle to Nozick.

Two other books may be recommended as treatments of particular themes. Alan Ryan's *Property and Political Theory* (1984) appeared when the present volume was substantially complete, and the text does not, therefore, draw attention to all the connections between the two. Ryan deals with problems about property through a discussion of attitudes to work and labour disclosed in the writings of some major theorists, giving a far more complete insight into the issues raised in Chapter 5 of this introduction. The articles which preceded the book, listed in the bibliography, will also be found very helpful. Lawrence C. Becker's *Property Rights – Philosophic Foundations* (1977) provides the only overview of attempts to justify private property, and some sceptical responses, all of which are subjected to critical scrutiny. Most are found wanting.

The *Nomos* collection of essays, *Property*, edited by J. Chapman and R. Pennock (1980) explores a number of themes, and the volume contains an extensive bibliography. Another collection which looks at property from several perspectives is edited by Peter Hollowell, *Property and Social Relations* (1982).

The bibliography in this book should enable the reader to follow up any particular interest. Where possible, it includes recent works on aspects of 'property' which provide their own bibliographical leads. But 'property' is an element in a great many discussions, which, with the exception of the works mentioned, have not been brought together in recent books dedicated to the subject. In the case of some notions of property, much has wrongly been taken for granted. The works listed will provide the best available link between the present introductory discussion and more advanced study. Two books which are valuable in pursuit of a more specialised understanding are James Tully's *A Discourse on Property – John Locke and his critics* (1980) and Richard Tuck's *Natural Rights Theories – their origin and development* (1979). Both raise questions about property beyond the historical limits of their immediate concerns, although both are fairly technical and will be more accessible to the reader who has looked at the material already mentioned.

Bibliography

Ackerman, Bruce A. (1980) *Social Justice in the Liberal State* (New Haven: Yale University Press).

Anselm of Canterbury (1974) *Monologion*, vol. 1, ed. and trans. Jasper Hopkins and Herbert Richardson (London: SCM Press).

Arendt, Hannah (1958) *The Human Condition* (Chicago: University of Chicago Press).

Arendt, Hannah (1961) *Between Past and Future* (London: Faber).

Aristotle (1962) *The Politics*, trans. T. A. Sinclair (Harmondsworth: Penguin).

Avineri, Shlomo (1972) *Hegel's Theory of the Modern State* (Cambridge: Cambridge University Press).

Aylmer, G. E. (1980) 'The Meaning and Definition of "Property" in Seventeenth-Century England', *Past and Present*, no. 86, pp.87–97.

Baker, C. Edwin (1975) 'The Ideology of the Economic Analysis of Law', *Philosophy and Public Affairs*, vol. 5, pp.3–48.

Baker, J. H. (1971) *An Introduction to English Legal History* (London: Butterworths).

Barry, Brian (1965) *Political Argument* (London: Routledge & Kegan Paul).

Barry, Brian (1973) *The Liberal Theory of Justice* (Oxford: Clarendon Press).

Barry, Brian (1977) 'Justice Between Generations', in P. M. S. Hacker and J. Raz (eds), *Law, Morality and Society* (Oxford: Clarendon Press), pp.268–84.

Barry, Brian (1980) 'Is it better to be powerful or lucky?', in *Political Studies*, vol. 28, part 1, pp.183–94; part 2, pp.338–52.

Becker, Lawrence C. (1977) *Property Rights – Philosophic Foundations* (London: Routledge & Kegan Paul).

Bentham, Jeremy (1911) *The Theory of Legislation*, trans. R. Hildreth (London: Kegan Paul, Trench, Trübner & Co.).

Berki, R. N. (1975) *Socialism* (London: Dent).

Berg, Maxine (1980) *The Machinery Question and the Making of Political Economy* (Cambridge: Cambridge University Press).

Berlin, Isaiah (1969) 'Two Concepts of Liberty', in *Four Essays on Liberty* (Oxford: Oxford University Press), pp.118–72.

Bock, Kenneth (1979) 'Theories of Progress, Development, Evolution', in

Tom Bottomore and Robert Nisbet (eds), *A History of Sociological Analysis* (London: Heinemann), pp.39–79.

Bonfield, Lloyd (1983) *Marriage Settlements 1601–1740: the adoption of the strict settlement* (Cambridge: Cambridge University Press).

Boyce, D. George (1982) *Nationalism in Ireland* (London: Croom Helm).

Bradley, Ian and Howard, Michael (eds) (1982) *Classical and Marxian Political Economy* (London: Macmillan).

Brenkert, George C. (1980) 'Freedom and Private Property in Marx', in Marshall Cohen, Thomas Nagel and Thomas Scanlon (eds), *Marx, Justice, and History* (Princeton: Princeton University Press), pp.80–105.

Brittan, Samuel (1977) *The Economic Consequences of Democracy* (London: Temple Smith).

Burke, Edmund (1906) *The Works of Edmund Burke*, vol. 2 (London: Oxford University Press).

Burke, Edmund (1910) *Reflections on the Revolution in France* (London: Dent).

Buchanan, Allen E. (1982) *Marx and Justice* (London: Methuen).

Buchanan, James (1975) *The Limits of Liberty* (Chicago: University of Chicago Press).

Carver, Terrel (1982) *Marx's Social Theory* (Oxford: Oxford University Press).

Chapman, John and Pennock, Roland (eds) (1980) *Nomos XXII: Property* (Chicago: Aldine Atherton).

Clarke, Simon (1982) *Marx, Marginalism and Modern Sociology* (London: Macmillan).

Coase, R. H. (1960) 'The Problem of Social Cost', *Journal of Law and Economics*, vol. 3, pp.1–44.

Cohen, G. A. (1978) *Marx's Theory of History – A Defence* (Oxford: Clarendon Press).

Cohen, G. A. (1979) 'Capitalism, Freedom and the Proletariat' in Alan Ryan (ed.), *The Idea of Freedom – Essays Presented to Sir Isaiah Berlin* (Oxford: Oxford University Press), pp.9–25.

Cohen, G. A. (1980) 'The Labor Theory of Value and the Concept of Exploitation', in Marshall Cohen, Thomas Nagel and Thomas Scanlon (eds), *Marx, Justice and History* (Princeton: Princeton University Press), pp.135–55.

Coleman, Janet (1983) 'Medieval Discussions of Property: *Ratio* and *Dominium* according to John of Paris and Marsilius of Padua', *History of Political Thought*, vol. 4, pp.209–28.

Connolly, William E. (1983) *The Terms of Political Discourse*, 2nd edn (Oxford, Martin Robertson).

Cullen, Bernard (1979) *Hegel's Social and Political Thought – an Introduction* (London: Gill and Macmillan).

Daniels, Norman (ed.) (1975) *Reading Rawls* (Oxford: Blackwell).

Day, J. P. (1966) 'Locke on Property', *Philosophical Quarterly*, vol. 16, pp.207–19.

Demsetz, Harold (1966) 'Some Aspects of Property Rights', *Journal of Law and Economics*, vol. 9, pp.61–70.

Dias, R. W. M. (1976) *Jurisprudence*, 4th edn (London: Butterworths).

Dickson, P. G. M. (1967) *The Financial Revolution in England: A Study in the Development of Public Credit* (London: Macmillan).

Drury, S. B. (1982) 'Locke and Nozick on Property', *Political Studies*, vol. 30, pp.28–41.

Elster, Jon (1978) 'Exploring Exploitation', *Journal of Peace Research*, vol. 15, pp.3–17.

Evans, Michael (1975) *Karl Marx* (London: George Allen & Unwin).

Filmer, Sir Robert (1949) *Patriarcha and other Political Works*, ed. Peter Laslett (Oxford: Blackwell).

Finer, S. E. (1952) 'Patronage and the Public Service', *Public Administration*, vol. 30, pp.329–60.

Finley, M. I. (1980) *Ancient Slavery and Modern Ideology* (Harmondsworth: Penguin).

Flathman, R. (1976) *The Practice of Rights* (Cambridge: Cambridge University Press).

Freymond, Jacques (ed.) (1962) *La Première Internationale – Recueil de documents*, vol. 2 (Geneva: E. Droz).

Furniss, Norman (1978) 'Property Rights and Democratic Socialism', *Political Studies*, vol. 26, pp.450–61.

Furubotn, Eirik G., and Pejovich, Svetozar (1972) 'Property Rights and Economic Theory: A Survey of Recent Literature', *Journal of Economic Literature*, vol. 10, pp.1137–62.

Gaitskell, Hugh (1956) *Socialism and Nationalisation*, Fabian Tract no. 300 (London: The Fabian Society).

Geras, Norman (1983) *Marx and Human Nature: Refutation of a Legend* (London: Verso/NLB).

Gill, Emily R. (1983) 'Property and Liberal Goals', *Journal of Politics*, vol. 45, pp.675–95.

Goodin, Robert E. (1982) *Political Theory and Public Policy* (London: University of Chicago Press).

Green, T. H. (1931) *Lectures on the Principles of Political Obligation* (London: Longmans, Green & Co.).

Grotius, Hugo (1853) *De Jure Belli et Pacis*, ed. W. Whewell (Cambridge: Cambridge University Press) 3 vols.

Halliday, R. J. (1976) *John Stuart Mill* (London: George Allen & Unwin).

Hansard (1822) Second Series, vol. 7.

Hansard (1823) Second Series, vol. 8.

Hart, H. L. A. (1955) 'Are there any natural rights?', *Philosophical Review*, vol. 64, pp.175–91.

Hayek, F. A. (1960) *The Constitution of Liberty* (London: Routledge & Kegan Paul).

Hayek, F. A. (1982) *Law, Legislation and Liberty* (London: Routledge & Kegan Paul).

Hegel, G. W. F. (1949) *The Phenomenology of Mind*, trans. James Baillie, 2nd edn (London: George Allen & Unwin).

Hirschon, Renée (ed.) (1984) *Women and Property – Women as Property* (London: Croom Helm).

Hobbes, Thomas (n.d.) *Leviathan*, ed. Michael Oakeshott (Oxford: Blackwell).

Hodgskin, Thomas (1832) *The Natural and Artificial Right of Property Contrasted* (London: B. Steil).

Hohfeld, W. N. (1919) *Fundamental Legal Conceptions as Applied in Judicial Reasoning* (New Haven, Conn.: Yale University Press).

Holcombe, Lee (1983) *Wives and Property: Reform of the Married Women's Property Law in Nineteenth-Century England* (Oxford: Martin Robertson).

Holdsworth, W. S. (1937) *A History of English Law*, 2nd edn (London: Sweet & Maxwell), vol. 7.

Hollowell, Peter (ed.) (1982) *Property and Social Relations* (London: Heinemann).

Holmstrom, Nancy (1977) 'Exploitation', *Canadian Journal of Philosophy*, vol. 7, pp.353–69.

Honoré, A. M. (1961) 'Ownership' in A. G. Guest (ed.), *Oxford Essays in Jurisprudence* (Oxford: Oxford University Press), pp.107–47.

International Federation of Phonogram and Videogram Producers (1984) *The Case for a Home Taping Royalty* (London: IFPI).

Jessop, Bob (1982) *The Capitalist State – Marxist Theories and Methods* (Oxford: Martin Robertson).

Kenyon, T. A. (1983) 'The Problem of Freedom and Moral Behavior in Thomas More's Utopia', *Journal of the History of Philosophy*, vol. 31, pp.349–73.

Knox, T. M. (1952) *Hegel's Philosophy of Right* (Oxford: Clarendon Press).

Lafargue, Paul (1975) *The Evolution of Property from Savagery to Civilisation* (London: New Park Publications).

Large, Donald W. (1973) 'This Land is whose Land? Changing Concepts of Land as Property' *Wisconsin Law Review*, vol. 1973, pp.1039–1083.

Lawson, F. H. (1958) *An Introduction to the Law of Property* (Oxford: Clarendon Press).

Letourneau, Charles (1892) *Property – Its Origin and Development* (London: Walter Scott).

Lively, Jack (1976) 'The Limits of Exchange Theory', in Brian Barry (ed.), *Power and Political Theory: Some European Perspectives* (London: Wiley), pp.1–13.

Lively, Jack (1978) 'Pluralism and Consensus' in Pierre Birnbaum, Jack Lively and Geraint Parry (eds), *Democracy, Consensus and Social Contract* (London: Sage), pp.185–202.

Lively, Jack and Rees, John (eds) (1978) *Utilitarian Logic and Politics* (Oxford: Clarendon Press).

Locke, John (1810) 'Fundamental Constitutions of Carolina', in *Collected Works*.

Locke, John (1965) *Two Treatises of Government*, ed. Peter Laslett (New York: Mentor Books).

Loevinsohn, Ernest (1977) 'Liberty and the Redistribution of Property' *Philosophy and Public Affairs*, vol. 6, pp.226–39.

Long, D. G. (1979) 'Bentham on Property' in Anthony Parel and Thomas Flanagan (eds), *Theories of Property Aristotle to the Present* (Waterloo, Ontario: Wilfrid Laurier University Press), pp.221–54.

McCulloch, J. R. (1848) *A Treatise on the Succession to Property Vacant by Death* (London).

McDougal, Myres S. *et al.* (1963) 'The Enjoyment and Acquisition of Resources in Outer Space' *University of Pennsylvania Law Review*, vol. 111, pp.521–636.

Macpherson, C. B. (1962) *The Political Theory of Possessive Individualism* (Oxford: Clarendon Press).

Macpherson, C. B. (1973) *Democratic Theory* (Oxford: Clarendon Press).

Macpherson, C. B. (1978) *Property: Mainstream and Critical Positions* (Toronto: Toronto University Press).

Macpherson, C. B. (1980) *Burke* (Oxford: Oxford University Press).

Maguire, John (1978) *Marx's Theory of Politics* (Cambridge: Cambridge University Press).

Manley, John F. (1983) 'Neo-Pluralism: A Class Analysis of Pluralism I and Pluralism II', *American Political Science Review*, vol. 77, pp.368–83.

Manuel, Frank E. and Manuel, Fritzie P. (1979) *Utopian Thought in the Western World* (Oxford: Blackwell).

Marx, Karl and Engels, Friedrich (1973) 'The Demands of the Communist Party in Germany', in David Fernbach (ed.), *The Revolutions of 1848* (Harmondsworth: Penguin), pp.109–111.

Marx, Karl (1974) *Capital*, 3 vols. (London: Lawrence & Wishart).

Marx, Karl (1977) *Selected Writings*, ed. David McLellan (Oxford: Oxford University Press).

Mathie, W. (1978) 'Property in the Political Science of Aristotle', in Anthony Parel and Thomas Flanagan (eds), *Theories of Property Aristotle to the Present* (Waterloo, Ontario: Wilfrid Laurier University Press), pp.13–32.

Meek, R. L. (1976) *Social Science and the Ignoble Savage* (Cambridge: Cambridge University Press).

Menger, Anton (1899) *The Right to the Whole Produce of Labour – The Origin and Development of the Theory of the Labourer's Claim to the Whole Product of Industry* (London: Macmillan).

Miliband, Ralph (1969) *The State in Capitalist Society* (London: Weidenfeld & Nicolson).

Mill, Harriet Taylor (1983) *Enfranchisement of Women* (London: Virago).

Mill, James (1978) 'Essay on Government' in Jack Lively and John Rees (eds), *Utilitarian Logic and Politics* (Oxford: Clarendon Press), pp.53–95.

Mill, J. S. (1865) *The Principles of Political Economy*, 6th edn (London: Longmans, Green & Co.).

Mill, J. S. (1983) *The Subjection of Women* (London: Virago).

Miller, David (1976) *Social Justice* (Oxford: Clarendon Press).

Miller, David (1977) 'Socialism and the Market' *Political Theory*, vol. 5, pp.473–490.

Miller, David (1982) 'The Macpherson Version' *Political Studies*, vol. 30, pp.120–7.

Miller, David (1983) 'Linguistic Philosophy and Political Theory' in David Miller and Larry Seidentop (eds), *The Nature of Political Theory* (Oxford: Clarendon Press), pp.35–51.

Miller, David (1984) *Anarchism* (London: Dent).

Milsom, S. F. C. (1969) *Historical Foundations of the Common Law* (London: Butterworths).

Moore, Stanley (1980) 'Marx and Lenin as Historical Materialists' in Marshall Cohen, Thomas Nagel and Thomas Scanlon (eds) *Marx, Justice, and History* (Princeton: Princeton University Press), pp.211–34.

Newby, Howard *et al.* (1978) *Property, Paternalism and Power: Class Control in Rural England* (London: Hutchinson).

Nicholls, David (1975) *The Pluralist State* (London: Macmillan).

Nisbet, Robert (1976) *The Social Philosophers* (St Albans: Granada).

North, Douglass C. and Thomas, Robert Paul (1973) *The Rise of the Western World* (Cambridge: Cambridge University Press).

Noyes, C. Reinold (1936) *The Institution of Property* (New York: Longmans Green & Co.).

Nozick, Robert (1974) *Anarchy, State, and Utopia* (Oxford: Blackwell).

Olson, Mancur (1965) *The Logic of Collective Action* (Cambridge, Mass.: Harvard University Press).

Oppenheim, Felix (1981) *Political Concepts – A Reconstructionist Approach* (Oxford: Blackwell).

Parel, Anthony and Flanagan, Thomas (eds), (1979) *Theories of Property Aristotle to the Present* (Waterloo, Ontario: Wilfrid Laurier University Press).

Parfit, Derek (1984) *Reasons and Persons* (Oxford: Clarendon Press).

Parry, Geraint (1969) *Political Elites* (London: George Allen & Unwin).

Paul, Jeffrey (ed.) (1981) *Reading Nozick* (Oxford: Blackwell).

Pelling, Henry (ed.) (1954) *The Challenge of Socialism* (London: Adam & Charles Black).

Plant, Raymond (1980) 'Economic and Social Integration in Hegel's Political Philosophy' in Donald Phillip Verene (ed.), *Hegel's Social and Political Thought* (New Jersey: Humanities Press), pp.59–90.

Plant, Raymond (1984a) *Hegel*, 2nd edn (Oxford: Blackwell).

Plant, Raymond (1984b) *Equality, Markets and the State*, Fabian Tract no. 494 (London: The Fabian Society).

Pocock, J. G. A. (1975) *The Machiavellian Moment* (London: Princeton University Press).

Pocock, J. G. A. (1976) *The Political Works of James Harrington* (Cambridge: Cambridge University Press).

Pocock, J. G. A. (1979) 'The Mobility of Property and the Rise of Eighteenth-Century Political Sociology' in Anthony Parel and Thomas Flanagan (eds), *Theories of Property Aristotle to the Present* (Waterloo, Ontario: Wilfrid Laurier University Press), pp.141–66.

Posner, R. (1973) *Economic Analysis of Law* (Boston: Little, Brown).

Pryor, Frederick, L. (1973) *Property and Industrial Organisation in Communist and Capitalist Nations* (London: Indiana University Press).

Pufendorf, Samuel (1710) *Of the Law of Nature and Nations* trans. Basil Kennet (Oxford: Churchill & others).

Rawls, John (1972) *A Theory of Justice* (Oxford: Clarendon Press).

Reeve, Andrew (1980) 'The Meaning and Definition of "Property" in Seventeenth-Century England', *Past and Present* no. 89, pp.139–42.

Reeve, Andrew (1982) 'Political Obligation and the Strict Settlement', *Locke Newsletter* no. 13, pp.47–55.

Reeve, Andrew (1984) 'Harrington's Elusive Balance', *History of European Ideas*, vol. 5, pp.401–25.

Ritter, Joachim (1968) 'Personne et Propriété selon Hegel', *Archives de Philosophie*, vol. 31, pp.179–201.

Roemer, J. (1982) 'Property Relations vs. Surplus Value in Marxian Exploitation', *Philosophy and Public Affairs*, vol. 11, pp.281–313.

Rousseau, Jean-Jacques (1915) *Political Writings*, ed. C. E. Vaughan (Oxford: Blackwell) 2 vols.

Ryan, Alan (1974) *J. S. Mill* (London: Routledge & Kegan Paul).

Ryan, Alan (1982) 'The Romantic Theory of Ownership' in Peter Hollowell (ed.), *Property and Social Relations* (London: Heinemann), pp.52–68.

Ryan, Alan (1983a) 'Public and Private Property' in S. I. Benn and G. F. Gauss (eds), *Public and Private in Social Life* (London: Croom Helm), pp. 223–43.

Ryan, Alan (1983b) 'Property, Liberty and *On Liberty*' in A. Phillips Griffiths (ed.), *Of Liberty* (Cambridge: Cambridge University Press).

Ryan, Alan (1984a) *Property and Political Theory* (Oxford: Blackwell).

Ryan, Alan (1984b) 'Liberty and Socialism' in Ben Pimlott, (ed.), *Fabian Essays in Socialist Thought* (London: Heinemann), pp.101–116.

Schwartz, Pedro (1972) *The New Political Economy of J. S. Mill* (London: Weidenfeld & Nicolson).

Seliger, M. (1968) *The Liberal Politics of John Locke* (London: George Allen & Unwin).

Simpson, A. W. B. (1961) *An Introduction to the History of Land Law* (Oxford: Oxford University Press).

Simpson, A. W. B. (1965) 'The Equitable Doctrine of Consideration and the Law of Uses', *Toronto Law Journal*, vol. 16, pp.1–35.

Skinner, Andrew S. (1982) 'A Scottish Contribution to Marxist Sociology?', in Ian Bradley and Michael Howard (eds), *Classical and Marxian Political Economy* (London: Macmillan), pp.79–114.

Smith, Adam (1853) *The Theory of Moral Sentiments* (London: Henry Bohn).

Smith, Adam (1976) *An Inquiry into the Nature and Causes of the Wealth of Nations*, ed. R. H. Campbell and A. S. Skinner (Oxford: Clarendon Press) 2 vols.

Smith, Adam (1978) *Lectures on Jurisprudence* (Oxford: Oxford University Press).

Snare, Frank (1972) 'The Concept of Property', *American Philosophical Quarterly*, vol. 9, pp.200–206.

Southern, R. W. (1970) *Medieval Humanism and Other Studies* (Oxford: Blackwell).

Spencer, Herbert (1851) *Social Statics* (London).

Steiner, Hillel (1975) 'Individual Liberty', *Aristotelian Society Proceedings* vol. 75, pp.33–50.

Steiner, Hillel (1977a) 'The Structure of a Set of Compossible Rights', *Journal of Philosophy*, vol. 74, pp.67–75.

Steiner, Hillel (1977b) 'The Natural Right to the Means of Production', *Philosophical Quarterly*, vol. 27, pp.41–9.

Steiner, Hillel (1981) 'Liberty and Equality', *Political Studies*, vol. 29, pp.555–69.

Steiner, Hillel (1982) 'Land, Liberty and the Early Herbert Spencer', *History of Political Thought*, vol. 3, pp.513–33.

Steiner, Hillel (1984) 'A Liberal Theory of Exploitation', *Ethics*, vol. 94, pp.225–51.

Stillman, Peter G. (1980) 'Person, Property and Civil Society in the *Philosophy of Right*', in Donald Phillip Verene (ed.), *Hegel's Social and Political Thought* (New Jersey: Humanities Press), pp.103–17.

Teichgraeber, Richard (1977) 'Hegel on Property and Poverty', *Journal of the History of Ideas*, vol. 38, pp.47–64.

Ten, C. L. (1980) *Mill on Liberty* (Oxford: Clarendon Press).

Thirsk, Joan (1969) 'Younger Sons in the Seventeenth Century', *History*, vol. 54, pp.358–77.

Thirsk, Joan (1976) 'The Debate on European Customs of Inheritance', in Jack Goody, Joan Thirsk and E. P. Thompson (eds), *Family and Inheritance* (Cambridge: Cambridge University Press), pp.177–91.

Thomas, Keith (1983) *Man and the Natural World: Changing Attitudes in England, 1500–1800* (London: Allen Lane).

Tierney, Brian (1983) 'Tuck on Rights: Some Medieval Problems', *History of Political Thought*, vol. 4, pp.429–41.

Trasler, Gordon (1982) 'The Psychology of Ownership and Possession', in Peter Hollowell (ed.), *Property and Social Relations* (London: Heinemann), pp.52–68.

Tuck, Richard (1979) *Natural Rights Theories – Their Origin and Development* (Cambridge: Cambridge University Press).

Tully, James (1980) *A Discourse on Property – John Locke and His Adversaries* (Cambridge: Cambridge University Press).

Vaughn, Karen Iversen (1980) *John Locke: Economist and Social Scientist* (London: Athlone Press).

Waldron, Jeremy (1979) 'Enough and as Good Left for Others', *Philosophical Quarterly*, vol. 29, pp.319–28.

Waldron, Jeremy (1981) 'Locke's Account of Inheritance and Bequest', *Journal of the History of Philosophy*, vol. 19, pp.39–52.

Waldron, Jeremy (1982) 'The Turfs my Servant Has Cut', *Locke Newsletter*, no. 13, pp.9–20.

Williams, Howard (1977) 'Kant's theory of property', *Philosophical Quarterly*, vol. 27, pp.32–40.

Winstanley, Gerrard (1973) *The Law of Freedom and Other Writings*, ed.
  Christopher Hill (Harmondsworth: Penguin).
Woodhouse, A. S. P. (ed.) (1974) *Puritanism and Liberty*, 2nd edn (London:
  Dent).

Index